PRAISE FOR
TO LEAD IS TO
TEACH

WHAT ASSOCIATION LEADERS ARE SAYING —

"If Dr. Jim Mahoney played baseball, he would be batting cleanup. He's a master at adeptly laying out his insight and ideas and bringing it all home. In short, he is a leader among leaders."

RICK LEWIS, Chief Executive Officer, Ohio School Boards Association

"I have never known a better storyteller than Jim Mahoney. *To Lead Is to Teach* lays out thoughtful, time-tested, experience-driven lessons for how all of us who serve as leaders—in any capacity—can grow. As a 30-year social studies teacher and president of the largest labor union and education organization in our state, I found that every chapter gave me new insights on how I can build on my personal experience and strengths to grow as a leader myself.

SCOTT DIMAURO, President, Ohio Education Association

"Mahoney weaves together his personal life and professional experiences in a way that both engages and enlightens readers who want to improve their leadership styles. As a union leader, I appreciate the value he puts on teachers and the teaching profession and how he uses it as the basis for leadership across sectors. I recommend this book to anyone who wants to lead with purpose, passion, and a people-centered approach."

MELISSA CROPPER, President, Ohio Federation of Teachers

"*To Lead Is to Teach* is very thoughtful and full of passion about the endless boundaries of leadership. Just right for leaders looking for ways to encourage the importance of relationships when leading organizations. It will definitely be on my book study list for our organization. I wish I had read this 30 years ago!"

DOUG UTE, Executive Director, Ohio High School Athletic Association

"All of the great coaches say there's no better teacher than real game experience. Dr. Mahoney's book of 'real game' experience provides excellent lessons for educators and leaders who want to see execution and winning results. It should be a required read for beginners or anyone who wishes to lead classrooms or boardrooms."

RICHARD "DICK" MURRAY,
Executive Director, Coalition of Rural and Appalachian Schools

WHAT BUSINESS LEADERS ARE SAYING—

"Jim's passion for effective teaching and leading has been a gift for everyone who has had the privilege to be in his circle. *To Lead Is to Teach* broadens the gift. Read, enjoy, learn, and then implement the insights—your effectiveness will take a big step forward."

JIM QUIGLEY, Retired CEO of Deloitte

"Mahoney shares his personal journey from the classroom to the boardroom and discovers that success in either utilizes a fundamental and core set of common skills and attitudes easily learned by others."

CARL KOHRT, Retired CEO, Battelle Memorial Institute

"I was (and am) fortunate to serve on the board of directors of Battelle for Kids, where Jim served as CEO for 15 years with passion and excellence. What he has shared in this book are all of the things that made him an effective, empathetic, and successful leader. Teaching was the core of his leadership, and this book is an excellent story of leadership principles and tactics."

LARRY HILSHEIMER, Executive Vice President
and Chief Financial Officer, Greif, Inc.

WHAT SUPERINTENDENTS ARE SAYING—

"This collection of anecdotes provides an abundance of takeaways that are sure to benefit any leadership professional. Jim's storytelling ability is unsurpassed, making these narratives both relatable and entertaining, while providing a wealth of knowledge and application. There are many lessons and strategies to be gleaned between these two covers."

MATT DILLON, PH.D., Superintendent, Petal School District,
Petal, Mississippi; Mississippi Superintendent of the Year

"Jim distills the research, illustrates the findings with relatable anecdotes, and offers concrete practices that can improve leadership effectiveness for any school or business leader. This is a must-have book that can serve both aspiring and experienced leaders. I highly recommend it."

Stan Heffner, Retired State Superintendent of Public Instruction Ohio

"Far better than the handwritten notes I have taken over nearly two decades seeking to capture 'Mahoneyisms,' this book is thoughtfully written and organized well. In it you'll find a resource for aspiring leaders, established leaders, and experienced leaders, because all effective leaders seek and apply the wisdom of great leaders like Jim Mahoney!"

Alan Seibert, Superintendent, Salem City Schools, Salem, Virginia

WHAT PUBLIC SERVICE LEADERS ARE SAYING—

"Jim Mahoney is a master teacher and leader with a storyteller's genius for bringing life lessons alive. *To Lead Is to Teach* is filled with wonderful, actionable insights borne from deep knowledge about teaching, learning and leading."

Greg Browning, Former State of Ohio Budget Director and Past Chairman Ohio University Board of Trustees

"In *To Lead Is to Teach*, Jim Mahoney informs, entertains, and persuades the reader. The book is a compelling lesson about what is important in life and leadership. As a person who led a statewide law enforcement agency, a billion-dollar pension system, and 4,000 employees of a state cabinet department, I wish I had read this book before all those experiences."

John Born, Executive in Residence George Voinovich School of Leadership and Public Service, Ohio University and former Ohio Director of Public Safety

WHAT HIGHER EDUCATION FOLKS ARE SAYING—

"Jim Mahoney is a master storyteller. His book is chock-full of inspiring stories about teaching, leading, and living. I believe every educator will enjoy reading this valuable treasury of stories and strategies."

William Purkey, Distinguished Professor, University of North Carolina, Co-Founder, International Alliance for Invitational Education

"Jim Mahoney gave us all a gift by sharing his gifts—relationships, storytelling, and a profound understanding of what makes people want to give their best to a shared purpose. I wish I had read this 33 years ago when I started teaching, or at least 20 years ago when I took on my first leadership position. People will be better for reading it wherever they are in their professional and personal journey."

MARSHA LEWIS, MPA, PhD
Associate Professor and Sr. Associate Dean Emerita,
Ohio University's Voinovich School of Leadership and Public Affairs

WHAT FOUNDATION LEADERS ARE SAYING—

"Decades of proven experience validate Dr. Jim Mahoney as a master teacher and exceptional leader. Dr. Mahoney reveals the power of being a lifelong learner, and then shows how to amplify that power by offering his ultimate lesson....the best leaders, like excellent teachers, are committed to using all that they learn to bring out the best in others. His book models this and is a terrific read for anyone reflecting on their leadership."

DAN KEENAN, Executive Director, Martha Holden Jennings Foundation

"One of the best things about *To Lead Is to Teach* is you travel along with Dr. Mahoney through his career as he discovers ways to connect with, teach, and lead people. It is not an 'I have the answers' book as much as it is a 'let's discover leadership together' adventure. Whether in education or business, the practical and real-world examples bring home the importance of being a leader who builds relationships, communicates, and collaborates with everyone in their care."

BRIAN WAGNER, Executive Director,
Muskingum County Community Foundation

WHAT OTHERS ARE SAYING—

"Jim Mahoney's compelling new book chronicles his lifelong devotion to educating children and supporting frontline educators. His engaging personal stories provide valuable and hopeful insights for parents, community leaders and educators."

MARK REAL, Co-founder,
Children's Defense Fund-Ohio and KidsOhio.org

"The first part of the book is an amazing self account with inspiring reflections on Dr Jim Mahoney's life stories. Jim has become one of the most influential, inviting and passionate leaders of the field now!

"The second part of the book provides many practical and substantial ideas to apply to the 'people domain' of developing oneself, schools, and organizations. The 'Mahoney Three' provides very practical suggestions to apply in many settings. I would strongly recommend this valuable resource to all people to share and learn."

DR. PETER KH WONG, Ex-Chief Curriculum Development Officer of
Hong Kong Education Bureau and
advisor of International Alliance for Invitational Education

"Jim Mahoney writes as he talks—clearly, enthusiastically, engagingly and persuasively as a master storyteller. Laying out his personal journey draws you into his thinking, values, and passions, setting the stage for his lessons learned, backed by research."

DAVID E. CHESEBROUGH, Ed.D., President Emeritus, COSI

"'Mr. Mahoney' inspired students and the Lawrence community nonstop. Who DIDN'T want to participate in Pioneer day or spend Saturdays playing softball with the students?! It was all about the kids. Jim's book brought back the joy and spirit of those early days."

MOLLY NELSON, former teacher, Frontier Local Schools,
New Matamoras, Ohio

"When I met Jim in his early teaching days, many of us called him 'Coach' because of his enthusiasm working with students both in the classroom and on the basketball court. This instructional manual on leadership, perfectly illustrated with poignance and humor, reveals how to be a coach for a lifetime when working at all levels of interaction."

ROB WEIDENFELD, retired teacher and union leader

TO LEAD IS TO TEACH

Stories and Strategies from the **Classroom** to the **Boardroom**

JIM MAHONEY

proving
press

Book Design & Production:
Columbus Publishing Lab
www.ColumbusPublishingLab.com

Paperback ISBN: 978-1-63337-520-8
Hardback ISBN: 978-1-63337-531-4
E-Book ISBN:978-1-63337-521-5

Printed in the United States of America
1 3 5 7 9 10 8 6 4 2

TABLE OF CONTENTS

Dedicated with love to
my daughters Amy and Susan
and granddaughters Lucy and Maggie.

FOREWORD

PERHAPS THE WORDS of Alfred Lord Tennyson capture the life journey of Jim Mahoney. Said Tennyson in his poem *Ulysses*, "I am a part of all that I have met." When you read *To Lead Is to Teach*, you will sense the richness of Jim's life and the blending of experiences that occurred along the way. You will notice the learnings along his path that have forged the fundamental aspects of his life's work. Again and again, regardless of the setting, he has always been teaching others, promoting collaboration, resolving conflict, galvanizing others with common goals, encouraging performance, and genuinely embracing the work.

Jim's collection of experiences began in his childhood in rural Southeastern Ohio. Due to his father's work, he relocated to various settings for periods of time, occasionally staying behind with extended family. His formal education, k-12 through college, occurred in five states and included rural, suburban, and metropolitan locations. New settings and stories were absorbed into the tool kit and would provide perspectives and insights to be used for the rest of his life. From rural Ohio to Los Angeles, CA, from the classroom to the board room, he has experienced and integrated it all. *To Lead Is to Teach* is a rich, synergistic piece of writing that connects the dots and culminates with a plethora of widely applicable strategies for leaders at all levels.

Regardless of the various professional milestones he has achieved, Jim always describes his life's work as that of a teacher with his first classroom experience (1973) in Frontier Local Schools, a small, poor Appalachian school district along the Ohio River. Jim passionately engaged fifth through eighth graders in brainstorming and collaborative problem solving, inspiring them in ways that would impact them for the rest of their lives.

In one of many collaborative projects, the class buried a time capsule with artifacts from 1976. Rather than leaving it for future generations to un-cover, the class chose to dig up the capsule themselves at noon on July 4, 2000.

As Jim's 30-year colleague who assisted with the July 4 event, I watched in awe as his former students and their children and extended families ar-rived in pickup trucks carrying grills and folding chairs. In the front yard of a small, aged brick school, the aromas of the grilling permeated the air as people greeted each other. A giant Fourth of July picnic ensued, after which the capsule was dug up and people cheered. I witnessed Jim in action, a magnet engaging the students and their families, inviting them to recall their memories of the time capsule project. The interactions clearly exhibited the strength of relationships and the value of collaboration, celebrating the completion of a project. The degree to which his now adult students were attracted to him spoke to the culture of caring he had created.

As Tennyson might say, each of those students was a part of what Jim had met, but more profound to me on that day was how Jim had become a lasting part of their lives too—not just in the moment he was their teacher, but in who they had become. They were the beginning of many who would meet and be impacted by Jim.

He soon applied his foundational classroom learnings to "office" and board rooms with the roles of two principalships, two superintendencies, and ultimately founding executive director of a not-for-profit, Battelle for Kids. He embraced the challenge of creating a self-sustaining business, learning new leadership lessons, and practicing old ideas that work.

You will come away from this book feeling more hopeful that YOU can do the work. You will read these stories and think of your own. You will absorb the lessons and repurpose them in your own life. They will become a part of what you have met.

Barbara Hansen, PhD
Dave Longaberger Professor of Teaching and Learning,
Muskingum University

INTRODUCTION

The first forty years of life give us the text;
the next thirty supply the commentary on it.
ARTHUR SCHOPENHAUER

I'VE HAD THE GOOD FORTUNE to serve as a teacher, principal, central office staffer, superintendent, college professor, and executive director. Looking back, I realize the best ideas I ever had usually came from others in the same role who were experiencing the same challenges and rewards—and sometimes heartbreak—as I was. In this book I share what I have learned as a catalyst for the learning of others, not a prescription for success. I certainly have had my share of failures as well. We all have to find our own path, but it sure helps to listen and learn from those who have walked similar ones before us.

This book is divided into two parts. Part I, the much smaller piece, is my short memoir of growing up, early influences, and learning the work of teaching, leading, and adapting. Part II includes useable, distilled lessons made possible by my experience and the best thinking and practices of many of today's current writers, thinkers, and researchers. At the end of each chapter are three actionable pieces that can be used by practitioners to introduce, reinforce, or teach the topic of that chapter. Each chapter in part II is a standalone topic in itself, worthy of much more discussion. Think of each chapter as a catalyst for the essential subjects in performing high-level work for teachers, administrators, or non-profit leaders. This is the work of leaders in classrooms and organizations.

In school, students get the lessons first, followed by the test. Life, of course, is just the opposite: You get the test first, and then the lessons. The main lesson I have learned again and again is that the extraordinary skills necessary to successfully engage students, motivate them, and support their emotional growth are the same ones necessary to lead adults. All the ideals we expect of a great teacher we expect of a great leader. If you can't teach, you can't lead anyone or anything.

I can clearly remember when I thought I ended my teaching career by taking my first principalship. I had a friend I knew loved teaching and was feeling the same spirit in his new role as middle school principal. One night at a local watering hole, he asked me to consider that maybe my classroom had simply expanded to include several hundred students and fifty some adults. That was the moment I realized I would always be a teacher. He was right. My assignment had changed, but the fundamentals were the same—teaching, promoting collaboration, resolving conflict, galvanizing others with common goals, encouraging performance, and genuinely embracing the work.

The same was true when I became superintendent and my class expanded yet again. The monthly board agenda became my lesson plan for the district. When I stepped into the role of founding executive director of a nonprofit organization, my teaching juices could not have been more alive as I created this new classroom with adults and students.

Teaching is leading and leading is teaching. One enables the success of the other. The two have become interchangeable to me. I have been doing both now for nearly fifty years. I've been blessed with energy and enthusiasm to do this work. Even after all these decades, it's still fun to start anew with a group of learners, ignite new ideas, and be a small part in the growth of others. Christa McAuliffe, our first teacher in space, had it right when she said, "I touch the future. I teach."

Part I

LIFE STORY

Chapter 1

RED BRICK HILL

Don't be afraid to be you and own it.
DANAE RINGELMANN

MY STORY AND LESSONS BEGIN with my own upbringing because we are, of course, all uniquely influenced by how we grew up.

As a small child, I lived with my paternal grandmother in Woodsfield, Ohio, in an area known as Boxtown. Some referred to it as "the hill"—from the top you could easily see the county courthouse and most of the town below. The hill was dominated by a few families known for poker games, one-time bootlegging, and more than a few young men who loved fist fighting.

My mother and father divorced when I was young. I never lived with my mother, who struggled with medical issues and alcoholism. My dad had custody of me, but I resided with numerous family members at different times, including three of his sisters (two were older and never had children). Multiple moves, different schools, and a variety of living arrangements were the norm for me. Dysfunction, family breakups, the death of my grandmother when I was ten, and other events along the way facilitated these moves. I was an energetic young boy, a challenge for them. Each would ask my dad to take me back after a time, and off I would go with him.

My dad was a machinist, and jobs were plentiful for him all over the country. After my grandmother passed away, I spent ages ten to seventeen in a whirlwind of places with interesting characters and, certainly, the unconditional love of a father. I know there were people who thought my dad should settle down and stay in one place. Repeatedly pawning me off to relatives and taking me back again seemed misguided to others. But that wasn't the way my dad lived. I unequivocally loved my dad, who made our trips into experiences, who always expected much of me, and whose encouragement fuels me to this day. What I remember best during my younger years are the long drives with just the two of us from Ohio to California and all the interesting places to see on Route 66 from St. Louis, Missouri, to Barstow, California.

One Saturday in the summer of 1960 when I was nine, my dad, who was visiting from Columbus, took me to the Western Auto to purchase my first two-wheel bicycle. It was red, and as I sat on the seat my toes barely touched the ground, keeping me balanced. I knew how to ride a bike, and my dad decided I needed a larger one that I could grow into over time. He let me ride it home from downtown, about a mile away. All was fine until I got to the bottom of "the hill": the road up was 600 feet of red brick, followed by a left turn and another 150 feet before you reached our house at the top. My dad yelled from his car window, "Pedal hard. You can do this!" And so I started up the long red brick hill.

As each pedal reached its top height, I pushed down hard, generating just enough force to keep the bike moving forward. I was standing up, pumping as hard as I could up the hill at a 45-degree angle. Each time I thought the bike was going to stop and fall sideways, I'd push through to keep the momentum going. My dad slowly followed in his 1959 black-and-white Ford Galaxy, encouraging me to keep pumping. Out of breath and red-faced,

I kept going until I made the left turn and finished at the top of the hill. I was both elated and tired when I hit the top in front of my grandmother's house. I had indeed pumped my bicycle the entire red brick hill!

This singular event is a metaphor for every obstacle I have ever faced. Born in that event was the notion that to develop confidence, you need to successfully complete something hard. That is still true today. If you want kids to have confidence, help them develop competence. The latter almost always precedes the former.

Pumping up the red brick hill was hard. And while I did the physical work myself, my journey was helped more than a little by the encouraging, insistent voice of my dad. "Keep going! Don't stop now! C'mon, boy, you are almost there." And then I was. His encouragement and support were always there, including his weekly calls during my first year of college when I was afraid I wasn't ready for the challenging coursework. But it began with the red brick hill. That sense of real accomplishment felt good.

The rest of my life I continued to climb other red brick hills. There have always been obstacles. But support shows you how, encouragement says you can, and confidence comes from overcoming the challenge. For me, it all started with the red brick hill.

Chapter 2

ANOTHER MOVE, ANOTHER SCHOOL

Bloom where you are planted.
SAINT FRANCIS DESALES

BECAUSE OF MY DAD'S WORK, I attended many schools across the country during my formative years, including stops in Wyoming, Pennsylvania, Arizona, California, and Ohio. All over the country we went. When I was in the eighth grade, we lived in Arizona for most of the winter with a World War II Army buddy of my dad's. In California we lived in an apartment and a rented trailer at different times. In those states I was enrolled in rural schools, suburban schools, and schools in large metropolitan centers, changing schools frequently during the same year. In my eighth grade year alone I began in a small rural school in Woodsfield, Ohio (population of 2,000), moved to a large suburban metro school just outside of Columbus, then to a school in Los Angeles, followed by a suburban school in Scottsdale, Arizona, and concluding the year back at the school in Columbus.

I distinctly remember moving to a large high school in Southern California from my small Appalachian high school in Eastern Ohio during my junior year. In Ohio I was mainstream in my burr haircut, blue jeans, pullover shirt, white socks, and Converse tennis shoes. When I appeared like that on my first day at Excelsior High School in California, I was an early version of E.T. to the rest of the class. I can still hear the laughter and see the smirks from my classmates. On top of that, I had to endure a well-intentioned geography teacher putting me on full display as she questioned me and showed everyone where Ohio was on the map. It might as well have been the moon!

And curriculum? I think the reason I loved history and eventually became a social studies teacher was because it was the only subject that stayed the same across state lines. American history was taught in the fifth grade, eighth grade, and eleventh grade. Government was almost always a senior course. Math and science were completely different matters, because small high schools often rotated their order. A student might take physics before chemistry, or geometry before Algebra II. It became a problem when I'd move while enrolled in geometry and the new school only had algebra to offer that year.

The ins and outs often left me very confused. As a junior I moved to a large city high school in Canton, Ohio, in the fall, approximately six weeks after school had started there. I ended up in a small honors physics class with all boys. I wasn't even on the same planet with them, but I had a wonderful physics teacher who helped me each night after school to make up for my obvious deficits. I have no doubt I learned more physics than anyone in that class because I started with so little. I also know I never scored above 60 percent on any test. I used to tell this story to my graduate classes without telling them the student was me. I would then ask, "What grade would you give this student? An A because he learned so much about physics? An F because he failed every test?" I will tell you what the teacher gave me: a C.

By my senior year, I had run out of relatives who would keep me. I wanted very much to spend my last year—an *entire* year—in the small school where my dad had grown up and where I had lived with my grandmother until she passed away. It happened only because my best friend in that town, Dave, asked his mom and dad if I could live with them during my senior year. They said yes, and in many respects that move was transformative to my life. The stability of that year was enormous, but even more important were the family practices I learned and witnessed firsthand—things many take for granted, but aren't realities for many kids—things like eating meals together at a regular time when everyone was expected to be there, sharing food, discussing the day, and helping clean up. There were regular bedtimes, dentist appointments (I had eight cavities the first time I went), and a host of things normal families did that I really had not learned.

Chapter 3

LOOKING BACK

I've learned that people will forget what you said, people will forget what you did, but people will never forget how you made them feel.
MAYA ANGELOU

IMAGINE THE YEAR IS 2045 and we are all attending a thirty-year reunion celebrating the class of 2015. Think students will remember if the state instituted new accountability rules that year? Or if students took end-of-course exams via iPads? Maybe, but probably not. What will they remember? Teachers, and more specifically the people who interacted with them on a daily basis and elicited feelings from them. They may not remember a single lecture from a social studies teacher, but they might easily recall his enthusiasm because they felt it and joined in with genuine interest.

I don't know who taught me how to read, fostered my love of learning, or insisted that I know multiplication facts. But I do remember the coach who let me join a basketball team just as the season was starting with players vastly superior to those I had played with at my prior school. I also remember being one of three students in the sixth grade who didn't go on the class train trip to Washington, DC, because no one could afford to send me. And

I'll never forget the teacher in Los Angeles who embarrassed me as a young transfer student from rural Ohio. Those memories are still fresh more than fifty years later. Think these things don't last and influence us? Teachers have more social and emotional impact than we realize.

This is not to minimize the knowledge and skills teachers pass on—they are critical building blocks for any student. But they are not sufficient. What good is it to make three years of academic progress in math if you never want to do another math problem? Emotional growth—resilience, grit, and perseverance—may matter as much as academic growth. Even today, as I take a mental trip to all the places I lived as a kid, schools I attended, and teachers I had, I recall those who inspired me and built a relationship with me, even if it was very short term. It mattered to my growth and development as a student and later as an educator as well.

I learned a lot about versatility, perseverance, and resilience as I moved from one place and culture to another. I also came to appreciate the simple kindness of a warm welcome. And who were the kids who extended a hand in high school? I can tell you it was most often the outcasts, the ones likely to proffer a cigarette with the welcome. The good students rarely were the welcoming ones; they were waiting, judging, trying to determine if I really measured up. All of this factored into my own teaching. Whenever I got a new student, I quietly welcomed him in the hall, got to know him, and never put him on the spot or, worse yet, displayed him in front of the classroom.

Turns out, all experience is cumulative and factors into the rest of your life. I didn't realize at the time that every move gave me a unique perspective and seeded insights that I would use later as a teacher, coach, administrator, and manager. By the time I reached college I had attended rural, suburban, and city schools in Ohio, Pennsylvania, and California. So, while I wasn't rich in money or stability, I hit the jackpot in sheer variety during my formative years. I went to school with Latinos, Native Americans, African Americans, affluent suburbanites, and small-town rural kids. I observed cultures up close and personal. I learned how to survive, how to be resilient, when to be smart and when to be quiet, and most of all how to fit in—all of which served me well later in life.

Chapter 4

COLLEGE STUDENT 1968-1972

In the depths of winter, I finally learned that within me
there lay an invincible summer.
ALBERT CAMUS

IT WAS WITH A MIXTURE of relief and anxiety that I began as
a freshman at The Ohio State University in the fall of 1968. I was relieved
that I could stay in one school for four years and anxious about whether I
was adequately prepared for college work. My anxiety affected me in other
ways too. My first history class was taught at the College of Law. Rather
than go the direct route from our rooming house through campus, I walked
the long way around the perimeter because I was afraid I'd get lost in the
large campus and never make it to class. This is just one illustration of all
that I didn't understand, wasn't prepared for, or was too afraid to try in this
unfamiliar land.

I was fortunate to have a support group in the form of two guys who
were a year ahead of me and shared my rooming house north of campus.
They showed me the ropes—where buildings were located, classes to take or
avoid, and the bars that were friendly to coeds. It was quite an adjustment

coming from a small rural high school during my senior year to a university with fifty thousand students.

I was so naive, even though I had lived in so many places. My first math class was taught on television by the author of the textbook we used. His name was Dr. Riner, and I couldn't figure out how he found time to teach math in between seeing patients. I had never heard of a PhD; the only doctor I ever knew was the one who gave me a quick physical for basketball in high school. Years later when I told that story, someone said to me, "You couldn't have been that dumb." I wasn't that dumb, but I was that naive. Kids don't know what they don't know. How can we expect students to imagine having an occupation they've never heard of, in a field they never knew existed, working across the globe with people they've never met?

That first year I learned another college classroom practice I hadn't known about previously: norm-referenced testing. In all the schools I had attended, teachers used fixed percentages for letter grades A through F: generally 90 to 100 percent earns an A, 80 to 90 percent earns a B, and so forth. If everyone scored less than 60 percent on a test, everyone failed; the less effective instructor would blame the entire class, while the more effective one would figure out whether it was their methods, course content, or the test itself that contributed to the dismal results. Grading in college was different. Whoever got the highest grade got an A, and the rest were scaled downward from there. I didn't need to know a prescribed set of content. I just needed to know more than most of the others in the class to get a good grade.

One night before finals, I was at a campus watering hole with two friends. We stayed out too late, and one wondered aloud if I was worried about the exam we had coming the next morning. I laughed and answered, "Of course, but a little less so than you two, whom I know I can score higher than on the final!" I always remembered that when I gave tests to students.

If it's really about learning—not judging and sorting—then students should get second chances or additional time to learn something.

My full participation in Army ROTC showed me a different approach to learning. No norm-referenced testing there. You couldn't just shoot better than other poor performers. No, now you had to demonstrate competency at standard levels of performance. And if you couldn't, you got more practice, more drills, more of whatever it took to get you where you needed to be. Years later as a superintendent of schools, I often remarked that the only standards-based environment I ever worked in was the US Army. No instructor ever said to me, "Some of you will get it and do it successfully and others won't." What they said was, "You will all get it eventually because that is our expectation for you." Why? Because there were real-world implications for our learning. Imagine being in a foxhole under attack when your buddy tells you he failed to learn how to load and reload his weapon after it ran out of ammunition.

ROTC taught me something else: the importance of mission and contributing to something bigger than myself. I've often said that if I got to be the Czar of Education, I would require all eighteen-year-olds to give a year of national service after high school. It would not have to be in the military and could include a variety of service opportunities. A year of service is the rent we should pay to live in a free country. It enables young adults to gain another year of maturity, mix with others different from them, and learn to contribute. How important is contribution? According to researcher Adam Grant, contribution can boost our confidence. He found that while gratitude is passive and makes us thankful for what we receive, contribution is active, boosts our confidence, and reminds us that we can make a difference.

Chapter 5

TEACHER
1973-1980

[Kids] don't remember what you try to teach them.
They remember what you are.
JIM HENSON

EFFECTIVE TEACHING is an emotional, physical, intellectual, and existential effort. Taking responsibility for another's learning—whether stepping in front of just one or hundreds of people looking to you to provide an engaging and meaningful lesson—is daunting. You don't realize how much it takes until you do it.

When I started teaching in the fall of 1973, I couldn't have imagined the many opportunities that lay ahead for me. I began my career as a classroom teacher in Frontier Local Schools, a small, poor Appalachian school district along the Ohio River. And yet it was in this context that I found my true calling, developed my own strengths, and began my preparation for myriad leadership roles later in life.

Proving that timing is everything, I was driving by the district office when I decided on a whim to stop and complete an application. As it turned out, the superintendent was there and wanted to see me. He needed a junior high teacher and basketball coach. He asked me if I had lettered in high school basketball (Thank goodness he didn't ask if I had played much or was any good!) and whether I could manage kids. I answered "yes" to both, and he offered me the job. I left the building walking on air, knowing I was returning to Appalachia to teach in a small school tucked into the Wayne National Forest.

My assignment that fall was to coach the junior high boys basketball team and teach fifth- through eighth-grade social studies, seventh- and eighth-grade physical education, and health. I lived in a small trailer twenty miles away in a remote wooded area. My first day I drove the thirty-five minutes to school on the single-lane highway, snaking up and down around curves and steep hills, and promptly went to the bathroom to throw up—likely a combination of nerves and motion sickness.

I remember my first day of school well, walking to my classroom on the second floor to meet my first group of students. The school was built in 1928, and the wood floors smelled of wax. I can still see the small river running fifty yards beyond the window panes. Desks were attached to chairs and could be opened from the top. My desk was at the front. All eyes centered on me as I peered at the group of twenty-six students and we all wondered what each would think of the other. I think it was in that moment that I fell in love with my profession. I had learned from my dad the difference between being *interesting* and being *interested*. I tried to do both as I introduced myself and they introduced themselves to me. I knew that I had an opportunity to make a difference in the lives of young people by what I did or didn't do, by what I said or didn't say, and by what I modeled or didn't model.

I remember seeing kids who looked like me, even more so when I was young: white, rural, mostly poor, sitting up at their desks, smiles on their faces, wondering what this new young teacher would be like but also willing to give me a chance. In my entire career I was never more respected, fairly treated, and honored for my work than during the seven years I taught school at Frontier. And while I'm not sure I had any parents with a college degree, I had adults blessed with common sense, a strong work ethic, and generosity of heart. If you "did right" by their kids, they would "do right" by you. I saw firsthand the old adage played out—people don't care how much you know until they know how much you care.

It probably wasn't possible to teach anywhere in America, and certainly in Ohio, and be paid less than what I made. And while I was jealous of my high school friends who earned twice my salary in the coal mines and aluminum plants on the Ohio River, I often thought how lucky I was that anyone would pay me anything to do something I thoroughly enjoyed. It was challenging, motivating, frustrating, confusing—and sometimes those feelings all came before noon. It required all my energy, wit, and creativity to stay up with all those classroom preparations and individual kids.

I had ownership, not accountability. I had creativity, not tools. I had respect, not compliance. I taught approximately 110 students in grades five through eight, many of whom I had all four years. (It was looping before we had a technical term for it.) I was responsible for teaching them the history of our state, our country, and the world. I had to figure out learning targets, ways to measure if kids had achieved them, and what to do next whether they did or didn't. I had no materials (not even teacher edition books), so I had to rely on my own creativity to create lessons that were engaging and useful. I knew my kids well, especially after teaching them for several years. I knew all their parents, and they trusted me to do right by their kids.

I was happiest when students were fully engaged with me. I loved brainstorming with them to get ideas, expand on alternatives, or just think together about a problem. Everyone participated, energy was created, and enthusiasm was heightened. My students learned they could offer ideas without my judgment, and because of that, ideas came more quickly and easily over time. Embedded in all those ideas were usually seeds to plant. While I loved the excitement of generating ideas, I equally liked the execution of ideas—to see something come to fruition. Sometimes education reformers tout project-based learning as if it were some new idea. Nonsense. There have always been teachers turning ideas into projects with multiple applications for learning. One of my former students said it best: What he remembered most were "ideas popping up everywhere." Those were among my most engaged and happiest times teaching school.

My favorite mantra in developing lessons came from this old proverb: "What I hear, I forget. What I see, I remember. What I do, I understand." Social studies lessons are notorious for reading, discussing some of what is read, and doing worksheets. If that is all it is, we could hire grandmothers to do a terrific job of that and building relationships to boot. Teaching is figuring out what we want students to know, be able to do, and show that they can do.

For example, my first group of students learned how a bill becomes a law. Rather than making it a rote memorization feat, we decided to create a country, give it problems to be solved, and have students govern it and serve as legislators. The country was named Harmony, and I used this device for the next two years with the class. Harmony had a flag, geography, history, and all the rest. The class designed these components and used them all the time across curriculums. If we studied pollution in health, I'd give the problem to Harmony. A legislative study commission would be appointed to give a report and make recommendations to the House or Senate based upon their position. Eventually discussion and a vote would occur. One student (now an engineer) made us an electronic voting board so we could tally how legislators (the class) voted on a particular bill. This is project-based learning. Critical thinking, communication, and problem solving have gotten a lot of attention as twenty-first-century skills for students, but they were needed in the twentieth century too!

There was one project that consumed two years of my life, including one entire summer. This project grew out of complete naivety on my part. In the fall of 1974, I went to the county library to check out a copy of *Andrews History of Ohio* because I knew there were short histories of each township in Ohio's eighty-eight counties. And sure enough, I found a short description of Lawrence Township where I taught. There were a few paragraphs about the early history and settlement that I wanted to share with my seventh-grade Ohio history class in response to their query, "What was it like here a long time ago?" However, the librarian said that students in the 1950s sociology classes at Marietta College had written small books about each of the townships, which she had in the back room. She promptly brought them all out but couldn't find one about our township. I then went to the college and found them all again—minus the one about our township.

I took a couple of the books to show the class the next day, and of course we decided that we should write one. This was long before computer-based word processing or internet research. So began our journey that took nearly two years. We investigated township village records, read old newspaper microfiche, conducted eighteen oral interviews, visited the archives at the historical society, read countless church and old personal diaries, and followed countless leads. By the time we were done, the entire community had helped in some way. Just after Memorial Day and three days before school ended in 1976, our 156-page book, *The Wilderness that Became Lawrence,* was printed.

We went through every step together as a class—researching, following up on leads, going to cemeteries, writing, editing, footnoting, dismissing things we could not find a second source for, and on and on. Now you know why it took one whole summer and two school years! When it was completed, I took it to a printer, who convinced me that we should print four hundred books. I explained there weren't four hundred people in the entire community, including animals, but he said it would be more affordable to print more. So, four hundred it was, and I took them to school three days before these kids would be going home for the summer and then off to high school without me. I owed one thousand dollars—approximately one-sixth of my annual salary. I can assure you at the time I had neither a thousand dollars nor for that matter a hundred dollars. My class of twenty-four students set the price at four dollars each. Each of us needed to sell ten books to break even. Talk about real world finance! It doesn't get any more real or relevant than that. I didn't have a school activity account to pay for it, as I had done it all on my own with the class.

What happened? We sold all four hundred books in two days! The day after I passed out the books is one I will treasure forever. Our secretary said there was a line of senior citizens downstairs who wanted their books signed! We printed another six hundred books and sold those. I went from worrying how to pay a bill to making sure the school got all the money and I could show all the records. Twenty years later and long after I moved out of town, I still got calls from people who wanted a copy of the book, most doing genealogy projects or they had descendants from the area. This is project-based learning—not a new concept at all.

The year *The Wilderness that Became Lawrence* was published (1976) was also America's Bicentennial. For a social studies teacher, this offered all sorts of interesting things to revisit in American history. That spring an industrial supply company provided a large time capsule for me to use with the class. As we studied artifacts from the Revolutionary War era, we filled our time capsule with current cultural artifacts that someone might dig up in a hundred years—from Carter/Mondale stickers (from that year's Democratic National ticket) to basketball uniforms and tests I had given students covering our study of the US Constitution. It was all great fun as we tried to imagine how others in the future might consider these items.

(That project became the topic of my master's work in history at Ohio University, where I met another teacher who became my wife the next year. We had two daughters, one of whom is a teacher today, so I guess we created our own tree of educators.)

I had these students for three years, and we had grown very close. In May, just before the end of school, one of my students said, "Hey, why don't we dig up this time capsule ourselves someday?" After some discussion, it was unanimous. We would bury it and choose a special, memorable time to reconvene as a class and dig it up, far enough in the future that we would want to come back. Someone else piped up, "Why not July 4, 2000? It's a date we all remember from our study of history, and it will be the beginning of a new century." And that is what we decided when we buried our time capsule. We—a class of twenty-four kids and their teacher—would reconvene nearly a quarter of a century later to dig up our artifacts and remember our shared time together.

I had a practice each year of having students write letters to themselves on the first day of school as if it were the last day of school. They would look at me and ask, "Whaaat?" and I would explain, "Tell me about your year. Who did you hang out with? What did you accomplish? What will you remember?" Then I'd collect their letters, promise to share them with no one, and give them back to them on the last day so they could see if their year had been what they thought it would be. Of course, I read the letters. When I passed them out at the end of the year I'd ask, "Who had something come true?" Nearly everyone raised their hands, and then I would explain a term I didn't use in the fall when they wrote the letter: goal setting. If you dream it, think it, and, most importantly, write it down, you have a much better chance of accomplishing it. And so I made sure that my students wrote letters to themselves to place in the time capsule, on top.

Those early years are best characterized as staying just ahead of the posse. If it was Tuesday, thinking about Thursday was long-range planning. Because I taught in the countryside and lived there as well, teaching was both my professional and social life. I mean, it wasn't like I spent my evenings at fine-dining restaurants and clubs. There were none of those things, which was probably good because I couldn't have afforded them anyhow. Instead, I focused all my energies at school. When basketball started, I was busy almost every night from mid-October through mid-February. That spring I added the role of assistant baseball coach at the high school to my responsibilities.

On top of that, one weekend a month I would rent a roller skating rink in Marietta, the county seat, as a fundraiser and social activity. Many families brought their kids, went grocery shopping afterward, and made this a special time. I loved it because I got to see all the kids in a different venue, got to know their families better, and really enjoyed an evening together. It wasn't an obligation. It was a fun way to build relationships for a young teacher who didn't have much else to do, and again, couldn't have afforded much else. I got to skate for free.

As I look back now, I see that this community served as a family for me. Both of my parents had passed away during those early teaching years, and with no siblings, I was bonding with students in ways that filled familial needs I had at the time. It was not unusual for parents to invite me to dinner at their house after practices or games. What I remember most, perhaps because I felt it so deeply, was their love and respect. I was not one of the kids. It was always "Mr. Mahoney." But those times when I skated with kids, pitched softball at recess, and stayed an extra hour after school for late buses—it was a labor of love. Do kids work harder in class for someone they believe cares about them, someone who goes the extra mile and asks questions about them? It is not rocket science. Relationships built honestly and authentically matter in business, government, and yes, in classrooms—especially classrooms.

Chapter 6
LESSONS LEARNED

Our fingerprints don't fade from the lives we touch.
JUDY BLOOM

AND NOW FOR THE TIME CAPSULE. I had my students write letters to themselves, imagining their lives in twenty-five years. I wrote a letter too, and prepared a cassette tape titled *In Case I'm Not Here*. I remember talking about what this group of kids meant to me after our three years together. Did they learn something about social studies with me? I hoped so, but what I hoped they would remember most was each other, our successful efforts to research and write a book, and the incredible camaraderie that was felt.

When the kids all graduated from high school four years later as part of a larger class with three feeder schools, I attended their graduation and gave each one of them an eighth-grade class picture with an inscription and invitation to be at our elementary school to dig up the time capsule on July 4, 2000.

In the spring of 2000, I met with four members of the class at a restaurant in Marietta to plan our July 4 reunion. I had not seen them for twenty years, not since they graduated from high school. As they walked in together to meet me, I recognized them but quickly added, "What happened? You all got old!" I'm happy to say they recognized me, and we sat down to plan our get-together. We decided to have a dinner at the school the night before for class members, and then at noon the next day we would dig up the time capsule and open it. The Jennings Foundation, a longtime supporter of Ohio teachers, agreed to fund the dinner if I would write an article for them about what I learned from the students nearly twenty-five years later.

I've attended hundreds of school dinners for good causes, but none was as special as that night in an old school gymnasium where I once coached basketball. Twenty-one of the original twenty-four students showed up. I brought three colleagues with me who asked each of the attending students a variety of questions during the two days. As for me, I just enjoyed seeing my students, their kids, and their parents—now grandparents. We talked, laughed, remembered, and simply enjoyed the time together as if time had been suspended.

Later that fall, I got a prompt from the Jennings Foundation that my article was due. I had not thought about it, but I did have many pages of transcribed tape from interviews my colleagues conducted with the students. I took the notebook and headed off to a coffee shop to read what they had said in preparation for writing the article.

On that dark, rainy afternoon, I slowly started to weep as I read all the comments. It was testimony to the fact that we can remember entirely different versions of the same event, or not remember certain things at all. I had no idea that I served as a father figure for one of the boys and that my interest in him made him work harder to please me. Or that an encouraging comment I had made in one instance and long forgotten was the centerpiece of what a student remembered about me all those years ago. It was a stark reminder that all things count, and I was taken aback that my actions—in many cases things that I had long forgotten—were important to them. What was also painfully evident from student interviews was not surprising: the content was not what they remembered more than twenty years later. Nobody talked about a social studies unit I spent forever planning, or the hundred-question test on the Constitution that I expected all students to pass. No. Five themes emerged from this learning experience, aspects of effective teaching that I have learned again and again. Below are some quotes from my former students:

Enthusiasm motivates everyone and is probably more caught and less taught.

"He was so enthusiastic. He would plant a seed. He didn't have all the ideas…there were just ideas popping up all over that classroom."

Engagement creates the best learning experiences.

"I think the big thing wasn't learning and memorizing facts. Like studying our country, he worked health into it…like there was an epidemic, and we had to figure out as Congressmen how to solve the epidemic. It is not so much that we remember history facts, but we remember the ways he made us remember them."

Equality contributes not only to a sense of fairness but also to a sense of family.

"He always treated everybody equally and it didn't matter how you were intellectually. He didn't let that affect the way he treated people and that has always stuck with me all through these years."

Expectations and feedback lessen misunderstanding.

"He's the one who always instilled in me the idea that whatever you

want to do, you can do it. Nobody can stop you….I guess I will always remember that."

Encouragement is oxygen to the soul. The need for approval and affirmation is universal.

"He made me think I could do anything I wanted to do."

I tend to remember what was pleasurable, what worked, and what made sense. I am far less likely to recall my short fits of anger, the times I sent an eraser flying toward someone not paying attention, or when I prepared lessons that just flopped. Did I always engage students? No. Sometimes I didn't know how. It's why today I ask educators to distinguish between the weather and the climate. I remembered the climate, not the everyday weather. My seven years teaching kids in Appalachia remain the most satisfying and happiest of my professional career. The lessons I learned, especially from this group of students with whom I spent three years, are timeless.

In our work lives it seems as if we have countless transactional moments but a very small number of transformational ones. I mean those instances in which your life or work is so changed by what happened that you never go back to where you were. Sometimes when the latter occurs you don't know it at the time. It's revealed later as you fully comprehend what happened, who you met, and how your life has changed. Professionally speaking, my first transformational moment occurred in the fall of 1979, when I actively participated in a teacher strike the first day of school. And while it was resolved on day two, lives and careers were dramatically changed for many in that episode.

It was also a time of particular unrest in Ohio, and school strikes in the '70s were quite common until legislation in the early '80s outlined collective bargaining rules. Suffice it to say that our district suffered from all those interpersonal wars between teachers, administrators, and board members. I can't remember all the details of the teacher strike that summer, but I remember how I felt just before and after the strike: disrespected, alienated, and divided. I have never talked to anyone who participated in a strike as a teacher or administrator who didn't remember the hard, divided feelings it leaves in its wake—especially in small rural communities like mine where everyone knows each other and people are forced to visibly take sides. Grievances became the norm, and whatever happened after the fact was seen as retribution or reward for where you stood on the school strike.

Although the school strike lasted one day, it might as well have been forever. Lines were drawn. Communities, families, and residents were divided. It was all very public. And while the issues have faded from my memory, the ramifications from that day have not. Our building was the only one in which half the staff actually showed up at school during the strike, leaving very bitter feelings when the other half returned a day later. People barely spoke to each other let alone collaborated. And while the other buildings didn't have that staff division, there was tremendous animosity from the staff toward the superintendent and principals.

At the end of the year of the strike, nearly one-third of the staff departed to seek employment in other districts. I was one of them.

Chapter 7

PRINCIPAL 1980-1983

Don't tell me what you believe. Show me what you do, and I
will tell you what you believe.
METEOR BLADES

IT TURNS OUT THAT ALL THE SKILLS I learned in teaching
were prerequisites to working in administration. I didn't "move up," as going
into school administration is often referred to by others. No, I had the opportunity to be a teacher in many new and different settings. I had no idea
back then that teaching middle schoolers or coaching high schoolers would
prepare me uniquely for the leadership roles ahead. The refrain of "I'm just
a teacher" turned out to be such a false moniker. A worse one—"Those who
can, do, and those who can't, teach"—was equally false.

I loved teaching. I couldn't imagine doing anything other than teaching
students about a subject I loved. In fact, when people asked me if I was going to get a principal's certificate, I said no. Principals, according to me, were
one of two kinds: teachers who couldn't teach successfully, or coaches who
had three losing seasons. (Of course, I exaggerate about all this, and on my
way to getting my master's I also attained a supervisor certificate that, with a

little work, I could turn into a principal's certificate.) I hesitated to consider a future administrative role because I enjoyed teaching so much. But a supervisor reminded me: "Jim, *administration* is taken from the term *minister*, which means 'to serve.' Administrative roles are another way of teaching, and really are servant leadership at its best." That framed it early for me, and he was right.

I was hired for my first principalship in an elementary school near Zanesville, Ohio, in a community more urban than rural. I was thrilled to have a new assignment, but I again suffered from all that I didn't know. I was the third principal hired in a short time; the former principal left me an envelope taped to the principal's desk entitled "to my successor." A two-page letter outlined by name and deed what an awful school I was about to lead. One teacher would do this, another teacher that, one of the school board members lived nearby and was a former principal who would offer more help than I needed. It went on and on.

I got back into my car and shared the letter with my wife, who promptly and correctly told me to tear the letter up and ignore it. At that time she had ten years of teaching experience with six different principals. She observed, "Do you think they were all good? Some were terrible. Make your own judgments, but if you keep that letter you will constantly look back at names to see if they are like what he describes rather than what you see and experience." Darn good advice and a lesson for the ages in leadership. I tore up the letter.

Most leadership roles are situational, and having the right skill set for the right situation is often the key to success. I wouldn't use a wrench to complete a job that requires a hammer, but we routinely do this by selecting leaders we like or those we think have earned a position, and not often enough considering whether they have the strengths to be successful in a given situation. While I don't know if this is what my employers thought about me at the time, this first principal role was a good match for me. The staff was hungry for someone enthusiastic, open, communicative, and honest about what they didn't know. (I was especially abundant in the last category, but filled in pretty well within the others, too.) It was a grand learning session for me to inherit 450 students and forty staff members in the K-6 building.

On a hot August day as I was opening boxes of new supplies, a relatively new teacher asked, "Is that what the principal should be doing?" I don't remember my answer, but I remember thinking, *I don't know what the principal should be doing. I'm just trying to make myself useful!* I met with teachers as they came in before school, introduced myself, got to know more about each of them, and listened to their views of what needed to be improved in the school. A couple teachers needed more textbooks, so I called the assistant superintendent to ask how I got more. She explained how to do a purchase order for the request, and then she hung up. I sat there for a couple minutes and then called her back. "What is a purchase order?" I asked. After a sigh and a laugh, she patiently explained that this was the statewide procedure to purchase anything for Ohio schools. I didn't know, because in seven years of teaching in one of the poorest districts in Ohio, I never purchased anything except with my own money. Teachers certainly didn't do purchase orders at my old school! And so my education on how to be a principal began.

My graduate program in history and administration had introduced me to organizational theory and covered the big issues of the time. But I wasn't prepared for the routine activities that ultimately define leadership. These activities, including my interactions with students, teachers, staff, and parents, slowly but surely defined me as a leader. I now realize I did some things right, others lousy, and somewhere along the way I got better. I do know this: it all counted and became part of how I am still remembered as a principal.

My second principalship was at a large middle school serving 725 students in grades five through eight in a small college town in eastern Ohio. I was hired just before the new school year after the principal left over some contentious events from the previous years. Once again I was helped by what I didn't know. I just liked middle school kids and jumped at the chance to lead a building with more kids and staff. By now I at least had a clearer picture of what a principal should do. I had been to "principal school" in real time and was ready for the next challenge.

My wife was at the local mall about six weeks after school started and overheard a conversation about me and the middle school. (In rural areas, when you return home from the mall your spouse is much more likely to ask, "Who did you see?" before any questions about purchases.) My wife was looking at dresses when a lady she didn't know ran into a friend she hadn't seen for a while. She asked how the new principal (me) was doing, how the school year was going, and so on. While my wife didn't know either person, she quickly realized from the conversation that one of the two ladies worked at the school where I was principal.

"Well, how is school with the new principal?" the first woman asked.

"It's very different," the teacher said.

"What does that mean?"

"There are just so many changes so quickly."

"Are the changes better for you and the students?"

"Yes, but it takes some time to get used to it. And the new guy isn't afraid to do things. But yes, things are improved."

My wife relayed the entire conversation while I asked questions to figure out who it was. I was happy that she thought the school was improved, even though she paused before she said it was better than before. This was sweet music to my ears, because all people, even principals, need affirmation, especially when they are changing many things.

My happiest days as a principal were the same as in teaching; I loved engaging the staff. My first assignment was student discipline. I'd been told numerous times that it was a problem. Getting people together, discussing ideas for improvement, launching a plan, and seeing it through were right up my alley. Later, as a middle school principal, I enjoyed devising an entirely different scheme for student organization that met their needs. Two years later, the school earned a blue ribbon and was honored in Washington, DC, as one of the nation's finest secondary schools. I was having fun.

Chapter 8

THE WRONG CHOICE

Anyone who has never made a mistake has
never tried anything new.
ALBERT EINSTEIN

MAKING MISTAKES provides a wellspring of lessons. A year after the strike, the superintendent in that school district announced that he was leaving. Even though I had only one year of experience as a principal, I was encouraged to apply for the job, and I foolishly did. Why? Because my heart was there. It was in my rural neck of the woods. I knew the families, loved their kids, and wanted to be back. On a 3-2 vote, I was selected to become the next superintendent. I accepted the position and began my job on a June morning. Complicating things were the aftershocks of the teacher strike that I had just been a part of little more than a year before. After spending the morning with the outgoing superintendent, I decided I had made a monumental mistake. Not because of anything he did or said, but because I knew I wasn't prepared for the role. I had teachers calling me to voice their support, two non-supportive principals who had wanted the job, and a school board split over me, even though the majority concurred with my selection.

How could all of this happened?

I was hired because I was a good teacher who did right by kids and families. I was very connected to the community because I loved my job and enjoyed reaching out, and not because I was priming for a loftier position. Remember, I was the guy who couldn't say the word *administrator* without a few expletives in front of it. The board and county superintendent never even called my references to see if my year as principal went well. They knew me as a teacher. So, for those folks who sometimes say, "I'm just a teacher," remember how powerfully your voice can be felt and your influence expanded.

On my second day on the job, I called the board president, a wonderful, sincere person in his sixties at the time. I had his nieces and nephews in school, worked with his sister, and was connected with the people in our part of the rural district he knew best. We met at a Burger Chef in Marietta.

"Mr. King," I began, "this is going to be a challenge, and I fear my very presence will continue this fight that started a year ago. Some teachers see my role as punishing principals, and some principals see my role that way too. I'm just not sure anything I do will really help the district."

He was so kind, probing me about goals and working with the board, but what I remember most was his sincerity and genuineness when he asked me, "Is this what is best for your family?"

At the time I had a wife and baby who were getting ready to move with me back to the area. Frankly, I didn't think my selection was good for anyone. I was conflicted about so many things—personal calls from teachers and parents, a board member's quote in the paper when I was hired, the former superintendent whispering in my ear that taking this job would be a mistake.

"Look," I said, "I accepted this role, and because of your confidence in me, I'll stay and do the best I can."

It was early June, and Mr. King said they had plenty of time to get another candidate. He let me out of it easily; I wrote a resignation letter right there at the Burger Chef. A few days later, the city's newspaper reported in banner headlines: "Superintendent Quits After One Day." It was true.

I called my former superintendent. Fortunately he had not named my replacement and hired me back. It was all very embarrassing, a bit shameful, and permanent. I officially burned one last bridge on the way out of town when I stopped to see one of the board members who had voted against me. She was quoted in the paper as saying, "The other candidates could walk circles around him!" I told her I had resigned and she could go get one of those circle walkers who were dying to take a job as superintendent in one of the poorest districts in Ohio and get paid less than I was going back to making for the principalship in my former district.

She was shocked and tried to talk me out of quitting. "We need you. I'll support you," she said.

"It's a little late," I reminded her. "You're already covered, aren't you? If I work hard and this turns out all right, it will be because you supported me. If it doesn't, well, you are already on record about that, aren't you?"

That was it.

I drove the seventy miles home and spent the summer regretting a bunch of things. But not the lessons. How many people have made a decision with their heart and not their head? It happens all the time. Mine just played out in a public arena. As an aside, they did hire a new superintendent. The board member who vilified me was defeated that fall, and a year later the district had yet another strike. But none of it justified what I had put myself and others through.

Chapter 9
SUPERINTENDENT 1983-2001

The greatest glory in living lies not in never falling,
but in rising every time we fall.
RALPH WALDO EMERSON

MY NEXT OPPORTUNITY to be a superintendent came five years later, after I had returned to principalship and spent three years as an assistant superintendent for East Muskingum Schools in eastern Ohio. Built in 1962, our high school was renamed to honor John Glenn, the patriot, astronaut, and former senator from Ohio who grew up there and attended our public schools.

The value of a trusted mentor is well documented. I had one of the best in Larry Miller, the East Muskingum Schools superintendent. One story in particular stands out as an example of the support I received from him. I had planned a county meeting of all teachers from six districts to learn together in a large city auditorium. I convinced my central office colleagues in other districts that we could attract better speakers, save money, encourage networking (though we didn't call it that then), and create excitement together. Everyone and their superintendents bought into the idea. Or so I thought.

When the day arrived, we packed a thousand teachers into an auditorium. Part of our goal that day was to have the Ohio Department of Education paint a vision for where the state was headed. This was a time when departments had respect from the field and represented the interests of students and educators at the state level, certainly long before state politics became the norm in education administration. Our state superintendent started the program out with a polished, clear overview of the state of education in Ohio. I felt good because I didn't think we ever could have gotten him and some of his staff to come to our neck of the woods with our small numbers. A great start. We should have stopped there. Things went downhill as each department official rattled on about technicalities and nuances that had little appeal or, frankly, applicability to most of the teachers. The rest of the day people gradually left the auditorium. Even my colleagues deserted me.

The next day, jokes circulated back in our district. Teachers made little paper badges that said "I stayed" and pinned them on their shirts. I quickly learned that unless you laugh at yourself, you leave the job to everyone else. I was humiliated, irritated, and convinced any large-scale collaboration between districts was gone forever. I dreaded meeting with my superintendent and mentor, Larry Miller, and admitting how poor the program was for teachers and how it reflected poorly on our county districts and, by proxy, the superintendents. He listened patiently and carefully as I outlined the day and the disaster that accompanied it. He asked pertinent questions for clarification and offered no judgment.

When I finished, he had two final questions that I have never forgotten. "If you were doing this over, what would you do differently?" And second, "What did you learn?" Then he offered this advice that I have carried with me since: "Remember, there are no failures, just lessons." In that moment he could have dampened my willingness as a young administrator to ever take a risk again. Instead, he made it a learning experience. It was a classic "failing forward" moment for me, long before we called it that, a gift from the personality and wisdom of a very smart leader.

I had the privilege of working with and learning from Larry for three years before he left to become county superintendent. Before he left he created a succession plan for the district. He never promised the job to me; he just taught me and prepared me to assume the role. Just as teacher education includes student teaching, I needed student administrating, and I got it under Larry Miller. It worked. The night he announced his decision to leave after nearly thirty years, I was hired almost immediately by the board as their next superintendent. This time, I did have some skill and experience, though honestly I wasn't entirely ready to follow in the footsteps of an icon in the community. But I was ready enough, confident enough, and still naive enough.

Being a superintendent was not like having a job or even a career. It was my life. Like leaders in many other positions, especially ones that serve the public, I was always on. People felt free to approach me at any time to inquire about a future possibility or just register some dissatisfaction with something or someone. You can't make up all the things that happen in schools—the controversies, drama, and unintended consequences of various events. If you aren't laughing every day, you aren't looking! While it could be exhausting, I also liked it because in those countless unscripted minutes I learned things I didn't know, built relationships that mattered later, and got to stomp out brush fires before they became forest fires. I had the privilege to build and enjoy a sense of community. I learned who to go to for help, who needed a helping hand, and what issues were on the horizon. The Irish have a phrase I love: "It is in the shelter of each other that people live." That is true regardless of district size, but it is amplified in smaller communities.

In the fall of 1988, we held a celebration for the future class of 2000. The kindergarteners wrote their aspirations for the next century on balloons that we launched from the high school practice field. We planted a tree to honor the class (which I replaced at least twice after droughts). Music teachers took their place at pianos while students assembled on risers to sing rehearsed songs. I had been superintendent for a little over a year.

While kids were assembling in the back rows, I asked the students if anyone knew who I was. One girl raised her hand. "You are Mr. Mahoney."

I was impressed that this child knew my name, so I pressed further. "Does anyone know what my job is?"

"You are the superintendent," another student replied.

I was pretty impressed that two five-year-olds knew my name and position, so I finished with one last question. (Everyone watched as they were all ready to perform.) "Does anyone know what the superintendent does?"

An excited boy's hand shot up. He shouted, "NOTHING!"

One of the kindergarten teachers next to me wryly added, "This is about the brightest group we have ever had."

We showed those videos at those students' senior assembly just before they graduated in 2000. I was there and so was the same kindergarten teacher, who affirmed her earlier remarks. It was the best (and some would argue most accurate) job description I was ever given!

Six years after completing my PhD in Educational Leadership and Administration, I left East Muskingum and took on the role of Muskingum County superintendent. In this role I advocated for a service to help our staff that eventually benefited me as well: I asked the board to approve a contract with a large hospital to provide support to people in special circumstances. If you had a recalcitrant teenager you suspected of drug use, this service provided one-time drug screening. If you had aging parents who needed counseling for a particular issue, they could get it. The cost was minimal, and the service was available to all staff members in all districts including secretaries, cooks, custodians, and bus drivers. Why? Because I wanted to communicate—build a culture, if you will—that we cared about the people who worked with children.

We understood that what happened in a person's life after work often impacted performance more than anything else. It's hard to focus on the task at hand if you are worried sick about your spouse or perhaps are in your own spiral of depression. I wanted to acknowledge that work is something you do while you also carry on the difficult task of living. This program acknowledged that at times we need help, privately, and it offered that help when staff needed it.

When I asked the board to approve the contract, one member remained skeptical but agreed with the caveat that we should review the policy in a year—not who used it, but how many times it had been used overall.

I interjected respectfully. "I don't think that tells us whether we should renew."

"Why not?" he asked.

I pulled my AAA card out of my wallet. "I purchase this each year and hope I never use it. In fact, it's a great year when I don't use it. But I continue to buy it for the security it provides me. It makes me feel good knowing I have it if I need it. This supplemental policy is intended to do the same thing for hundreds of adults. It says we care, and if they have special circumstances, this can help."

He smiled and said, "That makes sense."

I wanted to lead a culture of caring for employees. Do kids work harder for a teacher who cares? Do employees go the extra mile for an organization that cares? Yes.

Little did I know, I was going to tap into that service soon after we adopted it as I faced my own greatest challenge in life—sorrow and profound loss.

Chapter 10

PROFOUND LOSS

Life is like an onion. You peel it off one layer at a time,
and sometimes you weep.
CARL SANDBURG

MAY 22, 2001, began as any normal Sunday, the morning sun shining brightly as my youngest daughter, Susan, and my wife traveled by car to the large, brick-lined Presbyterian church about ten miles from our home. That morning I met with a half dozen junior high and high school students in a classroom underneath the sanctuary for our weekly class as I had for several years. If the truth be told, I taught the class because I enjoyed it more than the traditional service above me. I enjoyed talking with kids, leading a discussion about God, their lives, and lessons from the New Testament. Susan was sixteen and begrudgingly went with us most Sundays, including to my class. She was a typical teenager, alternating between excited engagement in the discussion and eye-rolling. Less than twelve hours later, our lives would be changed forever.

When bad things happen, we figure out, for the most part, how to "get through it." It's survival by whatever means necessary to get going, keep going. Only upon reflection much later, when the intensity of the pain has been relieved, can we begin to understand what happened and why we acted the way we did. We live forward, but we learn backward, as Søren Kierkegaard once said. And so it was for me.

Susan had been diagnosed with anorexia two years earlier. We watched her struggle with weight loss, anxiety, and energy bursts. She recovered (if one ever really does from this condition) after an intensive residential program where she regained weight, developed new coping strategies, and took on an adult maturity toward many issues. And yet the worry was always there. Anorexia isn't like a broken arm that gets repaired and heals. It is fundamentally a mental disorder that takes over your self image.

On this particular Sunday, Susan was upset that I had grounded her for attending a forbidden party the night before. A parent had called us that afternoon. I was upset. The drama heightened as I took away driving privileges first, berated her for going somewhere I had expressly forbidden her to be, and added a few more emotional hits. There was calm for a couple hours until she became sick. She began vomiting and told me she had taken some over-the-counter diet pills. We called 911 and rushed her to the local hospital where she had a heart attack and was life-flighted to Children's Hospital in Columbus. She passed away the next morning.

How can you go from a nondescript, lazy Sunday morning to the loss of a child in less than twenty-four hours? How can you ever go back, put one foot in front of the other, and even think of working again? I've done more than learn from profound loss; I've lived it. The unforgiving, searing pain never stops. Everything in my life became a sort of a.m. and p.m.: life before Susan died, and life afterward. Each time I went to a restaurant, wore a certain shirt, or saw someone we both knew, I said to myself, *The last time I ate here, wore this, talked to this person, Susan was alive.* A cascade of actions are set into motion with small and large implications for the rest of your life.

You learn to endure sincere but totally unhelpful messages: "Time will heal this"; "At least you still have another daughter"; "This is God's will and good will come from it." You realize that people support you until they don't; they go back to their lives while you remain frozen in time, stuck in an event that always has the same ending.

But eventually you do have to move—proactively, positively, and forward. And yet, not everyone can; not everyone does. Kübler-Ross's five stages of grief handily describe the process, but it isn't that simple when you're living it. There is a Jewish expression that says when a woman dies, the husband is a widower. When a man dies, the woman is a widow. When a child's parents die, the child is an orphan. But when a parent loses a child, there is no name for it because it is too terrible.

So how did I go from the death of my youngest daughter back to board meetings, directing and evaluating others, monitoring the progress of the organization, and all my other responsibilities? I changed from a "human being" to a "human doing." I just went through the motions. Less than three months later, I took another job with completely different people in another city, leaving behind my life and friends. That was my response. I didn't want to see people I knew. I didn't want to see the hurt in their eyes for me. I also felt like a complete failure as a father and, by default, as the leader of schools that help children. How could I possibly lead others when I had failed so miserably at home?

I quickly learned that new beginnings don't end the grief. You take it with you. And while time does reduce the intensity of grief, it never removes the loss. The immediate, unrelenting, indescribable pain is commensurate to the love you feel for someone. In a perverse sort of way, you are reminded through your sadness of your love.

I share this story as a reminder that we all have things that detract from our ability to perform at work effectively. We are always humans first. What we most need are leaders to support us, a culture to comfort us, and time to mend us. I found support from board members, colleagues, and friends, but the truth is that I checked out. As the lyric from "Hotel California" goes, "You can check out any time you like, but you can never leave." And so I found myself calling the grief line that was now available through our county district insurance, the insurance I had advocated for just a short time ago. I never thought it would be for me.

After Susan's death, my oldest daughter suggested through tears, "We need to remember Susan for who she was and not the disease she had." Susan was a gifted writer who journaled extensively and wrote several pieces her English teacher shared with me. And so, for nearly twenty years, our educational service center has awarded competitive Susan Writing Awards, a thousand-dollar prize, to nearly one hundred senior students. It has been helpful to us all to remember her in this small yet productive way.

Chapter 11

EXECUTIVE DIRECTOR NONPROFIT, 2001-2016

Never doubt that a small group of thoughtful,
committed citizens can change the world;
indeed, it's the only thing that ever has.
MARGARET MEAD

AFTER THE INCOMPREHENSIBLE LOSS of my daughter and my fifteenth year as a school superintendent, I received a call that changed my life. A consultant was searching for the first executive director of Battelle for Kids, a new organization to support school reforms that would improve student achievement in Ohio—a joint project of Battelle Memorial Institute (BMI), the world's largest not-for-profit, and the Ohio Business Roundtable (OBR), which is comprised of the CEOs of many of Ohio's largest and most influential businesses. I interviewed and was selected for the role. In October, I began my next fifteen years in the world of school reform on a larger scale, creating a self-sustaining business, learning new leadership lessons, and practicing old ideas that work in any setting.

While I'm not sure why I was hired, I know with certainty why I accepted the role. Aside from deeply personal reasons for leaving Muskingum County, I was attracted to the creative opportunity ahead of me. By then I had considerable experience working with school leaders as a service center superintendent and president of the Buckeye Association of School Administrators, Ohio's school superintendent organization.

Battelle for Kids was conceived with the idea that school achievement mattered and could be improved through the collection and effective use of student data by school leaders, increasing Ohio's standing relative to other states on the National Assessment of Educational Progress (NAEP). NAEP was commonly referred to as the nation's report card, because selected students from all states participated in this common measure. In 2001 Ohio was solidly in the middle of the pack, and our "big hairy audacious goal" was for Ohio to become first.

As the first executive director, I had the opportunity to frame the organization, hire staff, and help Battelle for Kids fulfill its promise to deliver higher results for Ohio's students. Little did I know when I accepted this position that all the skills I had developed as a teacher would once again be prerequisites for the role.

Our initial work was supported by ten million dollars of seed money, the largest investment BMI had ever made in a philanthropic project. I told people I felt like John Paul Getty, who once remarked that the secret of success was to get up early, work, and strike oil. Only this was not my oil. Gordon Battelle and his mother, Annie Maude Norton Battelle, founded the organization in 1929 with family monies and made education a philanthropic priority. They expected a return of benefits for Ohio's children. I was determined not to fritter away the large sum over three years and have nothing to show for it. I believed in my vision for Battelle for Kids, a vision I'd had to support during my interview process. The one-page vision statement I presented described an organization that looked strikingly similar to what it became, a testament to the fact that vision and focus matter in any new enterprise.

Part of my clarity came from my friend Dr. William Sanders, creator of the most reliable value-added metric in the country. Bill was a statistician professor and senior research fellow at the University of Tennessee in 1982. He learned about the attempts to introduce merit pay for teachers in Tennessee, and he developed the Tennessee Value-Added Assessment System, also known as the Educational Value-Added Assessment System, a method for measuring actual growth trajectories for students versus expected growth. This system became widely used across the entire United States and has been used to show how teacher quality is key to student achievement.

Bill and his team left the University of Tennessee to join the SAS Institute, the largest privately held software company in the world, founded by a colleague professor of Bill's, Dr. Jim Goodknight. SAS had the computing capability to scale his sophisticated methodology.

I went to Carey, North Carolina, to see Bill before my final interview with Battelle for Kids, because I wanted to see if he was willing to do what I wanted done, and if what I was asking was even possible. Because I had worked with Bill before on student analytics, I knew the power of measuring student progress and using that data as a tool for calibrating and driving student achievement. Our meeting occurred in late summer of 2001, before the passage of No Child Left Behind, the federal legislation requiring annual testing in grades three through eight. I can still hear Bill's voice describing the three conditions for computing a value-added score.

"Jim," he said, "school districts need to test children each year and tests must be reliable and positively, not perfectly, correlated to what you are teaching. So, to be crass, you can't teach German and test in Spanish."

He measured progress and that resonated with educators.

Frankly, then and now, we don't need tests to gauge school and district performance. Just review tax returns. There is overwhelming evidence that average family income is highly correlated to test results. And while achievement represents a point in time, progress measures the distance between two points. It was like my experience in high school physics: I got a C in the class but probably made the most progress because I had the furthest to go.

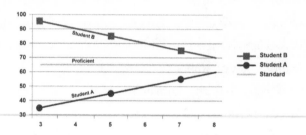

This napkin illustration explains the importance of measuring progress. I used to ask folks if they were buying a stock, would they pick A or B? Parents of high-performing students still want their children to make progress. Another napkin illustration I used was one depicting a two-by-two grid with achievement on one axis and progress on the other. Which school would you want your child to go to?

Progress and achievement are two different dimensions. Author and lecturer Doug Reeves describes these with 4 Ls: Lucky (high achievement, little progress), Losing (low achievement, low progress), Learning (low achievement, high progress), and Leading (high achievement, high progress). Pretty understandable, easily communicated, and largely accurate. Precise? No. And when we start tying individual teacher evaluations, salary, and other high stakes to these results, we create fear and demand that metrics do what they weren't intended to do.

Progress data resonated with me. Why would any educator go to a school with a preponderance of low-performing kids if accolades only went to schools with high performance? On the other hand, if we could measure real progress, acknowledge it, learn from it, and continue it, these teachers and students could reach higher levels of achievement over time. We needed data to spur student achievement, and Bill could give us that data. So in 2001, as the CEO of a new organization, I had an idea, a potential product, and even an innovative approach. But all that's nothing without customers.

I was attracted to the methodology Bill had been using and refining statewide in Tennessee because his approach was about improving, not simply judging. He had practical examples from educators on how the data and subsequent changes had transformed schools in Knox County, an early user of the new data. I was often asked why, if value-added data was so good, Tennessee wasn't leading the nation in NAEP and improvement. My response was always the same: a new thermostat doesn't make the room warmer, any more than weighing yourself helps you lose or gain weight. It's what you do with the information that matters. Dr. Sanders always argued for more effective professional development for educators.

Remember: context matters. The US was about to adopt what I'll call data-based decision-making for students. And non-educators were getting way ahead of themselves advocating for data-based teacher evaluation, salary, and school accountability. The question was: What data? Most states, with the notable exception of Tennessee, would continue to rely on achievement data, and No Child Left Behind (NCLB) codified it across the US. It was the national accountability piece of standards-based reform. The common narrative was that US schools were largely failing students; NCLB was sweeping legislation insisting that all students be proficient in mathematics and English language arts by 2014. Soon after the law passed, I was often asked whether I thought this would happen. My answer: No. While it turns out I was right, this wasn't exactly prophetic. But I never quibbled with the metric. Otherwise, schools might as well display a sign saying, "Welcome to

Any Elementary School. Some of the kids here will learn. Maybe yours will be one of them." I would further add, the real tragedy of performance is not failure to reach your goal. It's not expecting enough. Expectations matter, and reliable student progress data would help schools set goals and make changes that could measurably help students. These are lessons I had learned as a teacher, translated for nationwide applications.

Before NCLB, our team recruited forty-two school districts across Ohio who would allow SAS to calculate value-added data, pay attention to the results, and—most importantly—use the results to drive improvement. I had just finished a term as elected president of the Buckeye Association of School Administrators in 2000, and I personally knew most of the school superintendents in Ohio.

Battelle for Kids built a brand rooted in value-added data based on continuous improvement and the premise that working with school leaders increases achievement for students. Our proposition was pretty straightforward: measure something that hadn't been measured before—academic progress—and use this information with our help to accelerate improvement. We transformed an idea and a fledgling program in Ohio into a solid, high-performing, and self-sustaining not-for-profit organization working with districts and school leaders throughout the country. Our initial grant of ten million dollars was multiplied twenty-five times from 2004 (when we began seeking our own revenues) until 2016, in the form of grants, fees for service, and minimal philanthropic support. In those years we developed timely and useful products and services that were embraced by school leaders, including data tools, online courses, leadership training, communication services, and planned collaboration among school leaders. We created and supported the Ohio Appalachian Collaborative, which became a national model for rural collaboration, and met with Secretary of Education Arne Duncan to share its success and possibilities. Our myriad programs and efforts are well documented.

But what I'm most proud of are the countless relationships that made our work possible. While some pointed to higher achievement, larger revenues, or influential partnerships as metrics of success, I believe expanded opportunities for kids was the real metric. For example, students in Appalachia were able to take courses never before offered to them because of our work. Leaders improved strategies using data because of our training. Outstanding teachers were recognized by our state superintendent for the first time at state conferences we orchestrated. It was never about Battelle for Kids or taking credit. It was about helping others to be successful. That was our calling and our accomplishment. By 2015, Ohio was a top-ten state in the National Assessment of Educational Progress (NAEP).

While rising in the NAEP was rewarding, it wasn't what motivated me. I never worry about big hairy audacious goals that are consistent with the goals I am trying to reach. It's like coaching. Did I want to win games? Yes, every game I ever coached at any level. But I always believed that winning was a byproduct of doing other things right—creating cultures of hard work, focusing on effective practices, building team chemistry, and the like. And so it was with Battelle for Kids. If we did things right with people across Ohio, NAEP scores would improve.

Keep in mind, Battelle for Kids was not a business. We were a not-for-profit organization with considerable resources created to help districts improve student performance. We recruited superintendents from all types of districts in Ohio. This was not an urban, suburban, or rural effort. Too often reform strategies only impact a narrow cross section of kids—urban, poor, or another special category. Our aim was to improve performance in all districts for all students. We had large districts in our pilot pool (Columbus, Cleveland), suburban ones (Reynoldsburg, Bay Village), and rural districts (East Muskingum, Elmwood). We had a microcosm of Ohio—and the

USA. The table was now set. Implementing became easier once people saw the practical value of value-added data.

Let me give you a practical example from a conversation between two middle school principals. Both schools served affluent populations and had similar demographics. Both schools had high-achieving students. But the data revealed vast differences between schools in progress rates of seventh graders in science. The principals were friends who shared easily. The conversation went like this.

Principal A said, "Wow, look at your science scores. Collectively, all of your kids are making huge progress and certainly much more than mine. What are your teachers doing?"

The other principal smiled and said, "I'm going to give you a technical answer. I don't have a clue!"

With that we all laughed, but I asked the principal to follow up with teachers at his school and ask about what they were doing in science that might account for the tremendous student growth. He did and circled back with us. It turns out his four seventh grade teachers had divided the science curriculum; each teacher took one fourth and added experiments, activities, and substance to the lessons, specializing in the area they were most interested in teaching and developing. Then they rotated students between teachers for each new section. This was very early on in our project, and I was excited by what he had found out.

It was not that we had discovered the best approach to teaching seventh grade science, but we had discovered an effective approach—thanks to a conversation between principals using data they never had before. Prior to value-added data, both schools were high-achieving, and it would have been left at that. The data revealed something else that offered a chance at real improvement by teachers, revealed because these capable principals were able to have non-threatening conversations between themselves and with their staff about what was working. Improving is learning. It should not be threatening. My biggest disappointments came when value-added data was subsequently weaponized through its heavy use for teacher evaluation. It then became about proving, not improving. Still, effective leaders know how to distinguish noise from signal, how to lower the temperature, create conversations, and cultivate learning organizations for their staff and students.

As 2004 came to a close, our original ten-million-dollar grant from Battelle was winding down. We had firmly ensconced value-added calculations in the landscape, helped frame data-based improvement discussions throughout the state, and provided numerous schools with real improvement tools to increase student achievement. Our staff consisted of eight people who mostly had been there from the start. I assembled folks around our conference table with this blunt assessment: "We have done great work; assisted Ohio schools in real student improvement; and built some enduring relationships with districts, departments, and associations. We are running out of money, with enough resources left to pay people for six more months. What do you want to do?"

"What are our options?" they asked. "Is there a chance for another grant?"

That launched us into a candid discussion of possibilities. "It's unlikely," I answered, "that we would receive another large grant from Battelle, but I think they are still willing to support us on a much more limited basis, as they are pleased with our results."

"Can we seek other grants from businesses since this initiative was also part of the Ohio Business Roundtable?"

"We could, but I'm not sure we have anyone here with a skill set to do that kind of development. And personally, I'd rather do almost anything other than corporate begging of sorts—trying to explain to someone who doesn't really understand what you do why you want their money."

We bantered until the inevitable assertion was made. "We could be self-supporting through a combination of resources, including asking districts to pay for some of the services that we have been providing free of charge."

Our collective *aha* was now on the table.

I said, "Do we want to make it on our own, or tie a bow on what we have done up to now? Tie ends up and help everyone secure another job?"

Everyone present said, "I'm in."

Thus we had a new beginning, but one with a track record, a history of working together, and a unanimous belief that we were making a difference for students. A true story for the ages. Born in that conversation was a commitment from a handful of experienced professionals to stick around and give it their all. And when I retired after fifteen years, we were indeed still around. We generated resources from multiple sources, created a brand, and helped accelerate student achievement. Along the way, we sustained ourselves financially. From 2005 to 2016 when I retired, we had generated nearly $250 million in revenue. Not a bad story from any perspective.

While I was there, Battelle for Kids grew into a national not-for-profit that partners with school districts, state departments of education, business and philanthropic organizations in more than thirty states to advance educational equity and opportunity for all students. This work has impacted more than six million students and four hundred thousand educators nationwide.

That story could have ended differently. We could have tied the bow, celebrated our work, and moved to the pile of "do you remember when" efforts. As I write this, Battelle for Kids remains strong, and I hope it is a center for educational improvement for a long time. It started with that moment, that story of renewing commitments to do our work. My proudest accomplishment in those fifteen years is that the people in that room stayed for more than a decade, guiding, working, and creating as we went forward, willing Battelle for Kids to success. These weren't just the right people, but people who did things right. And they created a culture that attracted and kept people. On purpose.

Chapter 12

ASSISTANT PROFESSOR 2017-PRESENT

In my beginning is my end…
In my end is my beginning.
T.S. ELIOT

I NEVER TIRED of my work at Battelle for Kids. However, I did get tired from it. I spent the same number of years as their executive director as I had as a superintendent. It was simply time. And with significant cash reserves in hand, it seemed an opportune time for the next leader to make their handprint.

For me, it meant a return to the one thing for which I had never lost my love: teaching. Even in all my years as an administrator and CEO, I taught dozens of courses as an adjunct professor for multiple universities in Ohio. I still find it energizing to walk into a classroom of strangers and find ways to energize and engage them in their own learning.

I also enjoyed teaching about my most recent experiences. For example, in my first years as principal and central office administrator, I taught social studies methods courses to prospective teachers. As superintendent, I taught courses for folks pursuing principal licensure, and as an executive director, I taught classes on becoming a superintendent. So, as I concluded my service as a nonprofit leader, that was exactly what I wanted to teach. How does one become a more effective nonprofit leader? I chose this sector because I had relatable experiences, good and bad, to add to current knowledge, theory, and practice. Credible experiences matter.

I was fortunate to be offered a position at the George Voinovich School of Leadership and Public Affairs at Ohio University. In this role I teach nonprofit leadership and management to graduate students in public administration. I teach seminars on a variety of topics (change, motivation, strengths-based leadership, storytelling) to practicing public servants on behalf of a special Academy for Public Service attached to the school. My wonderful grandmother, who raised me until her untimely death when I was ten, would probably laugh if I told her people pay me to give keynote addresses now. She paid me five cents to be quiet as a youngster so I could buy an ice cream cone.

In the early 2000s, I taught a graduate class at Ohio State for students seeking their school superintendent licensure. I used a book, new at the time, by celebrated author and columnist Thomas Friedman. *The World Is Flat* argues that the world is being shrunk by technology, collaboration, and capital markets. Just a few years later, Friedman published another book reminding readers that when he wrote *The World Is Flat* the iPhone had not been invented, Twitter was a sound, apps were what kids completed to go to college, and the cloud was a meteorological condition. Now the world was really flat. The truth is it keeps getting flatter with newer connective technology, relationships spanning the globe, multinational businesses, and even the spread of an international virus. I loved using his books in the classroom because he paints a future of transformation. Friedman's contextual descriptions share a world in which you just know we are going to change forever how we do things and with whom we do them.

Yet the lessons I learned and apply in my teaching today are the same things I tried to do—unartfully but genuinely—nearly fifty years ago: find ways to connect to learners, learn with them, build relationships, and build a fire of enthusiasm and passion. I hope I do it today with more art and knowledge than I did with my middle schoolers in the '70s. The value proposition remains unchanged. Technology, pedagogy, and new information are available now, but it is still the teacher, the student, and the space in between. I still love mixing up the space in between.

Part II

LIFE LESSONS LEARNED

IN ALL THE ROLES I've had in education and the nonprofit world, there are certain truths that have emerged again and again. These truths are not always self-evident, so I share them here with stories and research that support the power of relationships, motivation, and culture.

I hope that new and seasoned teachers, administrators, and leaders find my experiences relatable and the lessons useful. I want my experiences—both joyful and painful, successes and challenges—to help others establish the most effective environment and culture to promote meaningful and productive schools and organizations.

Chapter 13

USE STORIES TO TEACH

Great stories happen to those who can tell them.
IRA GLASS

STORIES ARE POWERFUL TOOLS of inspiration, teaching, and communication of purpose. I realized the power of story when teaching middle schoolers, and applied that as an administrator and executive director. Why are stories so important? Because people remember them. When you hear a story, it becomes part of you. It becomes your story. Stories usually are associated with a lesson or moral that you want others to learn from and emulate. They can be illustrative, inspirational, and informational.

Life is a story with highs and lows, good characters and bad. It is always interesting. Our stories have been described as the window to our souls. In his book *The Storyteller's Secret*, author Carmine Gallo offers an observation I've made numerous times when testifying and watching testimony to state legislators: one emotional and vivid story is worth a gazillion PowerPoint slides. Stories are a critical block of communication.

I've never started a gathering of any sort without a story that illustrates a point or idea I want to talk about. Just watch the audience the next time you are with a speaker. When they launch into a story, ears perk up, cell phones go down, and interest soars. People love stories. But it's more than that. Stories are essential to persuade, teach, or apply an idea. As I've collected stories over the years that might be useful later, I put them in a box, and then two boxes, and then three and more.

Storytelling is the act of framing an idea as a narrative to inform, illustrate, or inspire.
CARMINE GALLO

Finding Stories

The best stories come from real life—your everyday experiences or those of others. I loved when teachers shared with me things that happened in classrooms; they provided a never-ending source of stories to make points, inspire others, and laugh together. You couldn't make up the things that actually happen in schools. When I first started as superintendent, an old hand suggested, "When you have twenty-three hundred kids interacting with two hundred adults all day after being bused a collective two thousand miles to get there, only a fool would expect this to go well!" He was right, of course. Stuff happens, some of it bad, but I learned that you always get to pick your response. And your response can calm it, escalate it, worsen it, lighten it—whatever *it* is. The event and the response together create the stories.

In any organization, stories come from the people who have worked there. I've given hundreds of convocation speeches to gatherings of educators. I almost always ask the superintendent who the past heroes or heroines are, who was respected, admired, known, honored—and why people felt that way. Then I connect those names and past deeds to points I want to make. It creates a powerful connection. Any new leader who doesn't acknowledge the value and people of substance from the past seriously overestimates their own importance. Honoring the past is a powerful motivator for those in the present. Find these stories and tell them. Share them through video, highlight them in newsletters, and tell them to groups, especially the entire organization. This is one way you teach, and above all else, a leader is a teacher.

In graduate classes, I often divided my class into teams and assigned each team a different book to read. I had them share their individual observations and key takeaways to their own team members first, then I formed new teams in which each person had read a different book. When I listened to these folks share their observations, they usually involved storytelling. Someone in the book lost everything to bankruptcy, found a new idea, and rose like a phoenix. By telling the story, they could illustrate the takeaway or lesson.

Crafting a Story and Presentation

Professional novelists and journalists make storytelling an art. Much of human history is told through stories. There are all kinds of genres and structures. When I think of a story that will teach a lesson, I try to think of these elements:

AUDIENCE. What about the story will be meaningful to the particular audience? What is the purpose of telling the story to this audience?

SINGLE MESSAGE. What is the message you want to get across? What is the lesson?

STRUCTURE. Who and what is the story about? How do the characters attempt to deal with the problem? How does it all turn out?

When I prepare a presentation filled with stories, for the sake of simplicity I always consider making three points so audiences can remember them easily. I ask three questions to help organize my presentation around three salient points:

- What do you want the audience to know?
- How do you want them to feel?
- What do you want them to do?

Each story must connect to its core message to be powerful. Don't tell too much. Overexplaining, overanalyzing, and overuse of acronyms are not limited to school leaders. When my youngest daughter was in the ninth grade she worked on a civics project. Each night she asked her mother for help, until the last night when I asked her point blank, "Susan, you know I used to be a social studies teacher. Why aren't you asking me for help?"

"Because, Dad, you would tell me more than I want to know."

Great lesson. Give people just enough, and make sure your stories and explanations make your presentation better, not worse.

Storytelling Lessons

Storytelling, according to Carmine Gallo, is the ultimate tool of persuasion. He suggests it is the coming together of ethos (credibility), logos (logic, data), and pathos (emotion). That's why it is so compelling and authentic when leaders tell personal stories. Take people on a journey describing imagery and detail. Don't be afraid to include mystery and curiosity because that keeps people with you.

One of the most watched TED talks of all time is from Sir Ken Robinson, who powerfully combined ethos, logos, and pathos in his argument for engaging students in education. He tells one particularly poignant story of Gillian Lynne, who was so fidgety as a child that school officials saw little hope for her. But a doctor told her mother in the 1930s (Sir Ken reminds the audience that ADHD wasn't an available condition then), "She isn't sick. She's a dancer! Take her to a dance school." There she met Andrew Lloyd Webber, and the rest is history. But Sir Ken uses this deeply moving story to think about students' creativity and natural gifts that we seem to destroy, even if not intentionally, over time.

I didn't know about storytelling at the time, but as a history teacher in the '70s I would challenge my kids to memorize any twenty words they came up with. I wrote them on the board until we had twenty. Then I made up an outrageous story using every word, erasing each after I used it. When all the words were used, I repeated the story with emphasis on the twenty words they chose. Then I'd challenge a student to tell the story. They could do it. Then I'd remind them that American history was a story. They wouldn't memorize it, but they'd remember it because it was interesting, instructive, and illustrative for our lives today. I was clearly doing storytelling a long time ago!

I often ask my graduate students to tell stories. They quickly remember their favorite ones about themselves or others; not just any stories, but ones that taught, inspired, or defined them. It's not unlike what I used to say to an aging history teacher when I was a young superintendent: "Ron, you don't teach history. You just remember it." We'd laugh. But people remember stories. Good leaders tell the right ones to fix points. Nelson Mandela had it right when he said, "Don't address their brains, address their hearts." It's exactly what good stories and storytellers do. Good stories can bring us to tears, motivate us to action, or save us from ourselves. Walt Disney added that storytellers "instill hope again, and again, and again."

Stories Build Purpose and Define Culture

Leaders who tell stories about their organization build purpose—they connect employees to a higher calling. As an example, Gallo tells the story of Howard Leonhardt, who invented the stent graft system used successfully to save lives in the treatment of cardiovascular disease. As CEO of his 200-person biotech company in Fort Lauderdale in 1997, Leonhardt received a 3:00 a.m. call from the Miami Cardiovascular Institute, asking to use one of Howard's stents to help a patient too weak for surgery—this application could save his life from a ruptured thoracic aneurysm. Howard agreed to get the stent from his office and bring it to Miami, about twenty miles away. Here was the catch: The patient was in Vienna, Austria. There was a 5:00 a.m. direct flight from Miami, and they believed they could keep the patient alive until Howard could get there with the stent. Howard grabbed several stent sizes from his office, caught the plane to Vienna, and rushed to the hospital there just a few hours later. After some difficulty, the surgeons successfully deployed the proper stent, sealed it, and the patient immediately began to stabilize. Howard got to meet the patient's German wife and daughter in the waiting room. Interpreters introduced him as the man who came from Miami to save their husband and father. With tear-filled eyes, they expressed gratitude to the man who had traveled all night.

When Howard returned to Florida, he shut down the plant to tell everyone what had happened. By relaying the story, which became the company story, he cemented the purpose of their work. He answered in bold terms what author Simon Sinek said is WHY we do things. Mission, purpose, and vision matter. Oliver Sacks said, "I can hardly imagine medicine without medical stories."

There are so many stories for teachers and leaders to mine, making them part of the fabric from which others learn, are motivated, and gain strength.

One of my favorites from my time at Battelle for Kids came from a tech/data guy we had working with the Houston Independent School District (ISD) when Hurricane Rita threatened the area shortly after Katrina. The district desperately needed a backup system in case of catastrophic loss of records, especially payroll. The Chief Technology Officer (CTO) at that time was a no-nonsense person who demanded results. Our guy on the ground was brilliant, guiding the CTO through all the steps—over a continuous twenty-four-hour period—to create and secure a functioning system.

The CTO wrote me an uncharacteristic letter praising our employee's efforts, acknowledging that he was the best she had ever worked with, and that he had worked under pressure to make it all happen. None of this was in our scope of work, so everything he did went above and beyond. Fortunately, Rita was underwhelming, but Houston ISD was prepared.

Suppose a team developed a new successful strategy or enlisted a new client. Let them share this story at a staff meeting. Think about it. First, do you think the client and especially the CTO are likely to continue services from Battelle for Kids? As a leader, is this what you want from people? Of course. And the story was a point of continuous inspiration and pride for everyone in the organization.

Lesser known but equally important to me was the story of our staff rallying around a young employee who beat breast cancer. These stories matter for the example they set and the culture they embed. Wise leaders use them. To illustrate. To initiate. To inspire.

When aren't you presenting to persuade, explain, or apply? Peter Guber, CEO of Mandalay Entertainment, argues, "If you can't tell it, you can't sell it." And must you be a celebrated inspirational speaker to do this? No. These are skills that can be taught, practiced, and improved. Consider the fascinating talk by Bill Gates during which he drank a glass of water that had been human waste five minutes before. Think he didn't have everyone's attention with that illustration, and have them ready to hear about the problems of sanitation, the importance of clean water, and what we can do to solve this problem for the world?

President John F. Kennedy, quoting journalist Edward R. Murrow of CBS News, said of Winston Churchill, "He mobilized the English language and sent it into battle." Churchill, in the space of a few months through a handful of speeches, persuaded a nation not to appease a dictator and ultimately saved not only his country but perhaps the free world.

Language. Emotion. Stories. Communication strategies, practice, and lessons should be required for every leader and student.

THE MAHONEY THREE

ONE: Divide people into small groups and ask them to think of a story to share. It can be one from their experience, or they can borrow stories from others—just be sure to give credit. The story should have a beginning, characters, and an end. Ask them to make sure they have a point in mind. What does the story illustrate? Then discuss how they might use that story in a larger context. For example, suppose someone offers a sterling story of integrity. A leader might use that story to highlight a new process they are instituting, or illustrate why an audit is so important. This exercise is an easy way to help people develop a habit of telling stories.

TWO: Host a story competition at your next staff meeting. For example, maybe you want folks to share their best customer service story from the past quarter. Place people in groups to share with each other, and have each group select their best story for the team entry. Then let groups tell their story to the entire staff, all of whom vote by applause. Give winning team members a small gift card to thank them. You want to inject a little fun while affirming something important to the organization—in this case customer service, but it could be a story to best illustrate your organization's mission or how teams work best. You affirm the behavior or feeling you want to reinforce by telling stories.

THREE: Start your own box of stories. They may come from *Reader's Digest*, a TED talk, or just everyday interactions with all sorts of people. Look for these opportunities, write them down, and place them in your box to be used when you have to give a presentation, introduce a concept, or write a short piece.

Chapter 14

LOVE WHAT YOU DO

**Find out what you like doing best
and get someone to pay you for it.**
KATHARINE WHITEHORN

AS I DESCRIBED EARLIER, my first teaching job was in a small, poor, Appalachian district in Southeastern Ohio. I used to laugh and say that I could not have taught anywhere in Ohio and made less money. Little did I know then that I had found my true calling.

After teaching, I went on to become a principal, superintendent, and then executive director. I found that each new position built on the solid foundation of skills and strategies I had developed as a teacher. I wanted my staff and all those who worked with me to trust me to do right by them, just as my kids had trusted me. In every position I had to determine achievement targets, ways to measure them, and what to do next whether we met the targets or not. I had to rely on my own creativity to create experiences that were interesting, engaging, and useful.

Just like when I was in the classroom, it was exciting to encounter problems, elicit creative approaches from staff, and then take action. I got so much from energizing groups, providing a little direction, and doing something to benefit others. Loving what I did and having a foundation in teaching made every endeavor so much easier, more engaging, and more fulfilling for me. Whenever a staff member came to me to discuss their retirement I'd say, "It's only work if you would rather be doing something else."

A disturbing study released by Strada and Gallup discovered that 51 percent of working adults would like a "do-over" to get a different degree and enter another line of work. That's pretty damning when you think of the costs and opportunities that get squandered because people don't get it right the first time or can't cross over to another profession.

The study suggests a gap year for students between high school and college as a good way to lessen the probability of a poor choice. I imagine a gap year not only for students of wealthy families—with unpaid internships, traveling abroad, and short, high-interest classes. No, I imagine a program where you can earn money, have multiple experiences, and buy a little time to figure out who you are and what you like and don't like. Private and public entities could help finance the program and secure real help. Just think if students had another year to do military training, participate in different experiences, and earn enough to make this possible. It's not a hammock but rather a safety net, a place to try and fall, understand yourself better, and figure out if your potential future is a good fit. Perhaps the gap year is really your senior year in high school.

The truth is, there are not very many seventeen- and eighteen-year-olds who know who they are and what they want to do. Sometimes we think the goal for students is to get a college degree or certificate. For most people, the degree is not the goal. It's the job! More often than not, you wind up somewhere because a friend worked there, a family member pointed out the job, or some other serendipitous event occurred. I was lucky to find a job I loved from the start. Most people aren't. But think of all the personal and organizational benefits to helping kids get it right earlier rather than later.

Because most people spend countless hours at work, a satisfying and fulfilling job will lead to a satisfying life. That's why it's so important to choose life paths that give you opportunities to find purpose, have autonomy, and develop mastery.

Your work is going to fill a large part of your life. And the only way to be truly satisfied is to do what you believe is great work. And the only way to do great work is to love what you do. If you haven't found it yet, keep looking, and don't settle. As with all matters of the heart, you'll know when you find it.

STEVE JOBS

Purpose, Autonomy, Mastery

While I can look back and see clearly what engaged me and made me happy in the past, it's all retrospective. The first time I took the Clifton StrengthsFinder 2.0 test in the mid-2000s, what did I learn about myself? I was an activator, relationship builder, and influencer. The things I enjoyed most about teaching in the early '70s were the same things that made me happy and productive in my later roles. It's who I am, and I have spent a lifetime building strengths from those early talents.

In his book *Drive*, Daniel Pink shares the research on what really motivates folks to excel and find meaning in their work. What gets them to do things in the first place? Purpose. Autonomy. Mastery. These three ideas, he argues, are the keys to motivation. The more motivated people are by them, the more likely they are to be successful and fulfilled in whatever they aim to do. Each of these key motivators has played a role in my own career.

PURPOSE is the yearning to do what we do in the service of something larger than ourselves. *Check.* It's why I got into education in the first place. I wanted to make a difference in people's lives. I didn't enter teaching to raise test scores, nor did I take the role at Battelle for Kids to raise NAEP scores. Scores aren't what got me going in the morning.

AUTONOMY is the urge to direct your own life. *Check.* I like calling plays and being held responsible for results. It's why I liked teaching so much. The freedom to innovate and solve problems was thoroughly motivating. I got to call plays every day. I decided whether we went on a field trip, read a certain book, or participated in an activity (consistent, of course, with my goals for students' learning). I relished the idea of calling plays in my later roles, and I pushed back when anyone tried to take play-calling away. Nobody wants to be the head coach if someone else calls the plays but holds you accountable for the results—unless of course the results are good, in which case the owner takes full credit.

MASTERY is the desire to get better and better at something that matters. *Check.* I had experience, wanted to test my theories on a bigger scale, and knew how to benchmark progress along the way. Looking back, I can see that Pink is right. These three factors are motivating and fit me perfectly in every phase of my career.

> Human beings have an innate inner drive to be autonomous, self-determined, and connected to one another. And when that drive is liberated, people achieve more and live richer lives.
>
> DANIEL H. PINK

Making Career Choices

Of course you can make wrong choices, as I did when I accepted my first superintendent job. I made a decision with my heart and not my head, then realized it would not be the best choice for me or my family.

This experience taught me an important lesson: don't apply for jobs only with your heart or because you want affirmation. Apply because you have spent time understanding what is expected of you and you want the position. That doesn't mean you can't decline if you are offered the job. But be of good intention in heart and head. Making the decision solely on one—heart or head—won't work. I could do that superintendent job now, but then I couldn't. The lesson is to know what you know and what you don't know. If you wait until you are totally prepared for a certain position, you may have waited too long. But you have to know enough. In my case, "very, very little" didn't cut it. But I was ready the next time.

A friend of mine says all the time, "Bloom where you are planted." You can do great work, be influential, and make an impact right where you are. Dan and Chip Heath, in their book *The Power of Moments*, outline a study of five thousand workers who assessed themselves for their level of passion and purpose for their work, where "passion" was defined as their excitement and interest in their work, and "purpose" was the degree to which they connected a higher sense of calling to what they did. Researchers then looked at where employees stood relative to performance. Who were the star performers? Unsurprisingly, those who had both passion and purpose were in the eightieth percentile for performance. Those with neither were in the tenth percentile.

But what if you could only pick one—purpose or passion—for your new employee? Which would be the most likely predictor of good performance? Turns out, if the employees in the study had purpose but not passion, they were still in the sixty-fourth percentile for performance, while those with only passion were in the twentieth percentile, barely above the "neither" group. Interesting research shows that people who have a deep sense of purpose and meaning in life are much healthier than those who find other types of happiness such as self-gratification. A meaningful and purposeful career has great potential to generate happiness and be more satisfying overall.

Purpose, autonomy, and mastery drove my decision to accept the position at Battelle for Kids. I had a creative challenge and the autonomy to frame the organization. My background as a teacher, principal, and superintendent gave me the experience I needed to succeed.

Finally, it is important to know when to move on. Sometimes that choice comes as an opportunity, like my offer from Battelle for Kids. When it becomes easier to take shortcuts, do what you've always done, and not ruffle feathers, it may be time to move on. This is true for any CEO, but especially for those in public service. Long tenures in the same role can endanger your sense of purpose, autonomy, and mastery—that intrinsic motivation to get better and better.

Bloom where you are planted, find yourself a trustworthy mentor, take risks, learn from your failures, and be of good intention in heart and head when you decide on a new position.

THE MAHONEY THREE

ONE: Purchase the book *StrengthsFinder 2.0* by Tom Rath and use the code inside it to take the CliftonStrengths Assessment, taken over twenty million times by individuals across the globe. Review your top five strengths and ask yourself, "Am I using these strengths in my everyday leadership? If not, how might I do that?" Gallup research has identified that people who use their strengths are simply more productive and seem to enjoy a higher quality of life.

TWO: Go directly to people you supervise or evaluate and ask them this question: "When you do a good job with something, how would you like me to reward or acknowledge that?" Some folks are motivated by public recognition, others by private notes. The point is to not assume that one size fits all or, worse, that folks are motivated by the same things that motivate you. It's a variation of the Golden Rule—treat people the way they want to be treated.

THREE: Perhaps nothing contributes more to your development than a mentor. Seek one out to learn from, connect with, and serve as a sounding board. Make it a real relationship over time. Leaders, especially successful ones, are happy to help others who ask them sincerely. Ask.

Chapter 15

MAKE RELATIONSHIPS MATTER MOST

It is in the shelter of each other that people live.
IRISH PROVERB

TEACHING IS A PROFESSION that involves developing relationships with students, parents, other teachers, and administrators. Those relationships are often difficult to build. A new teacher quickly finds that not every student loves them. Some parents blame the teacher for their child's struggles. Teachers may clash with other teachers, and they often do not agree with administrators. But over time, just as students find a way to adjust to different teaching styles, effective teachers find a way to develop relationships of mutual respect with all kinds of people.

Dr. James Comer, noted professor of Child Psychiatry at Yale, said succinctly, "No significant learning occurs without a significant relationship." He could have added "no significant business deals" or "no significant elections" or anything that involves people. Even those with technical skills (i.e., dentistry, roofing, estate planning) rarely find repeat business without building relationships. We like people who like us, engage us, and show a sincere interest in us.

Relationships are even a matter of life and death. One of the most famous longitudinal studies, the Harvard Study of Adult Development, followed 268 Harvard men over seventy-five years, beginning their sophomore year, to identify predictors of successful aging. Robert Waldinger, the current director of the study, suggested it could be summed up in one word: *love*. Even financial success, for example, depended upon warmth of relationships. And warmth of parental relationships predicted less anxiety and more life satisfaction.

Relationships continue long after someone passes on. Consider the poignant story that Kennesaw State University former president Betty Siegel tells about her husband, Joel. Joel grew up with his mom and grandmother in rural Kentucky until his grandmother passed away. He and his mother then moved to Louisville, where he began school as a third grader. He did not adjust well, and his parochial school teacher, Sister Agnes, often visited with Joel's mother about his behavior. Later that year, Sister Agnes said that she believed Joel's problem was his eyesight, and new glasses would help him to see, do schoolwork, and get along better. He got some, and by the end of the year, Joel was doing beautifully both academically and socially. He also did well in school later, graduating with high honors from high school and college.

Later, in a casual conversation with his mother, Joel remarked how funny it was that he had eyeglasses as an elementary student, but his eyesight grew better, and by junior high he didn't need them anymore. "Joel, you didn't need eyeglasses," his mother said. "Sister Agnes came to me with a plan to help you make a fresh start, and the glasses were a way to do that. It worked very well." Joel laughed. Sister Agnes, whom he loved very much, had given him exactly what he needed at that time in his life.

Fast forward another fifty years. Joel and his wife visited the grave of Sister Agnes shortly after he retired as a Georgia judge. He was on his knees softly praying and talking to Sister Agnes in the cemetery behind the church. "I need glasses now, as I've grown old. Thank you for all you did for me to set me straight, get me on the right path, and help me to believe in myself. I've never forgotten you." The people who help us in our formative years stay with us forever.

Your Relationship With Yourself

Perhaps the first relationship to build is with yourself.

Happiness is an indispensable ingredient in your success. In *The Happiness Advantage,* Shawn Achor argues that even the smallest shots of positivity can lead to competitive edges for us. He suggests several ways to boost overall happiness:

1. Meditate
2. Find something to look forward to
3. Commit conscious acts of kindness
4. Infuse positivity into your surroundings
5. Exercise
6. Spend money on experiences not stuff
7. Exercise a signature strength

Use this list to help yourself and others you work with daily. I found again and again that it is most often the little, simple things that matter most.

Martin Seligman, the father of today's positive psychology movement, in his book *Flourish,* says that the goal of positive psychology is to increase the amount of "flourishing" in your life. Flourishing comes from well-being, and the two, Seligman suggests, are interlocked and include five elements:

1. Positive emotion (feeling happy and satisfied)
2. Engagement (being completely absorbed by a task)
3. Relationships (finding ways to help others as an antidote to the downsides of life)
4. Meaning (believing in something bigger than yourself)
5. Accomplishment (taking pride in attaining goals)

Seligman offers a simple, compelling flourishing test. Is there someone you could call at 4:00 a.m. to talk to? If the answer is yes, you will likely live longer than someone who answers no. I would also suggest that you become the person someone might call at 4:00 a.m. Relationships are built piece by piece, person by person, over time. You rarely help someone else without helping yourself, too.

Related to these five elements are the characteristics of optimism, vitality, resilience, self-esteem, and self-determination. People who flourish have at least two of these five characteristics present in addition to the five elements listed above, according to Seligman. Building a positive relationship with yourself involves caring for yourself, but it also involves building meaningful relationships with others.

Relationships With Students

As a teacher on the first day of a new school year, especially if you are new to the school, you and your students start to get to know each other. You all decide if you can trust what you see and hear. Relationships bloom when you figure out classroom behaviors, establish expectations, and settle into the dance of teacher and students. We know students and teachers are more successful when they have positive and meaningful relationships. The five themes that emerged from my middle school time capsule project are key factors in building relationships with students at any grade level.

ENTHUSIASM

Your personal interest and enthusiasm energize the group and make others want to join too. Enthusiasm is like adding gasoline to the fire. As a teacher, I loved brainstorming with kids, listing ideas on the board, asking questions, and clarifying what was asked or discussed. Teaching without enthusiasm is akin to breathing in a room with little oxygen. Enthusiasm is motivating to everyone, and it is probably more caught and less taught. Keep learning fun, and find ways to make it relevant and memorable. Plant seeds of ideas for students (and staff) to nurture and grow. Create an environment where others want to join in.

Some people create what Seligman calls a positive "contagion of morale." Here is an example from the NBA. Seligman's group got all the sports pages quotes for members of NBA teams for an entire season, then blindly rated them for optimism or pessimism (not knowing what player or team the quote was attributed to). Optimistic teams were more likely to overcome a point spread; pessimistic teams were least likely to do so. And it held true for coaches too. Optimism helps spread positive morale. It is also associated with less risk of cardiovascular disease and even protection against the common cold. This is backed by science, not just happy people parsing out narratives. Passion is contagious too. You inspire and enthuse others with your own enthusiasm and passion. I used to silently laugh when I heard that so-and-so was burnt out. I wondered, "How can you be burnt out if you have never been lit?" Passion is your light, and it lights the room for others.

ENGAGEMENT

As a teacher, I tried to engage students in projects in which they were doing real things. I had to rely on my own creativity to build lessons that were both engaging and useful. My students probably don't remember worksheets they filled out, but they remembered researching our book, planning an annual

Pioneer Day for the entire community, and participating in the State History Day competition.

Sometimes I didn't know how to engage the class. Other times I realized I had to teach some content before they could start the project. For example, I couldn't give a mythical country a legislative problem to solve if I hadn't yet taught how our branches of government work at the state and federal levels.

I learned that pedagogy is important. Teachers can plan fun activities to engage kids all day or spend countless time sharing ignorance in cooperative groups. But students won't get anything out of it. Any meaningful activity requires a real connection to the learning objective in your curriculum. Too often I see teachers misinterpret activity for good pedagogy.

The Premack Principle works here. Given two activities, it's best to start with the activity that students prefer the least. Give them a preview of the enjoyable activity coming, but make them complete the low preference activity first. For example, I told my students the next time it snowed we would do fractions by drawing circles in the snow, but we couldn't do that until they first understood fractional parts.

EQUALITY AND CARING

Just about any class has a wide range of students—boys and girls, athletic and non-athletic, friendly and shy. I never consciously treated one group differently from another. Kids noticed they were treated fairly and mentioned it enough that I realized how important this was to them. I found that equality results in a sense of fairness and also a sense of family. I was never pressured to give certain kids more opportunities than others. "We," "us," and "our" come easier when students are encouraged to grow, play, and learn together.

Educators often ask the wrong questions. "Why don't kids get enough sleep?" "Why don't they have essential prior knowledge?" "Why can't they behave?" The fact is, these questions don't matter because a teacher can't go into the past and do anything about them. The right question is: "What am I going to change about it?" As educators, we can be irritated all we want about a kid who didn't get breakfast and comes to school hungry. But that student still comes to school hungry. It's why schools are now finally talking about dinner programs and providing weekend backpacks for kids who go home to places with no food over the weekend. To paraphrase Martin Luther King, Jr.: It's a little disingenuous to ask kids to pull themselves up by their boot-straps when they don't have boots.

Students need to see teachers practice what they preach. If you expect kids to be polite and respectful, then you need to model it. Try this: put your fore-finger together with your thumb to make a circle. Now ask people to make the same circle with their hands and place the circle on their chin. While you share these instructions, actually place the circle on your cheek. What will people do? Almost always they place their fingers not where you said (your chin), but rather where you showed them (your cheek). Monkey see, monkey do!

You can't fake it with students. They know, and what's more, remember if a teacher likes them or doesn't, if a teacher cares about their learning, improvement, success, and well-being. Accepting students as they are and treating everyone fairly is critical to building relationships. Students develop confidence and are grounded when their teachers love them just the way they are. Great teachers build relationships with their students by showing they care about them. They want them to succeed, and they support their interests and goals in and out of the classroom.

EXPECTATIONS

Few things are more researched and documented than the importance of teacher expectations for learning. I often ask new teachers to think of how their students will answer the question, "What does your teacher expect of you in terms of learning, behavior, or participation?" Students want to know. I also ask starting principals what they expect of teachers. People want to know! It shouldn't be a secret or, worse yet, never communicated until it's too late to do anything about it. People need specific, clear expectations and feedback.

With expectations comes support: students need opportunities for practice, coaching, and feedback. Otherwise, most students will not be able to learn and improve. Too often we make teaching and learning more about judgment than improvement. The purpose of assessment should be to improve, not prove. Improvement happens when you support expectations with help, feedback, and modeling. The literature is filled with examples of the importance of formative feedback. Treat somebody as if they were what you wanted them to be, and they become it.

There is a wonderful anecdote about Michelangelo. He purchased a large boulder from the local rock merchant and had it delivered to his home studio. The merchant didn't think it was a particularly good one and tried to talk him out of it. But Michelangelo insisted on it. Day after day he chipped away while a small boy watched over a fence. Slowly, *David* began to emerge in all his beauty from the rock. As Michelangelo was putting the finishing touches on his masterpiece, the small boy who had watched it all asked, "How did you know he was in there?" The most powerful teachers see in their students what the students don't see in themselves. And it begins with expectations.

ENCOURAGEMENT

Encouragement is gasoline to the engine. Of course, students work harder for someone who cares about them and offers positive feedback. This is not to say that teachers simply go up and down the rows encouraging and acknowledging kids for anything and everything. But look for ways to acknowledge progress and improvement.

The encouragement I received from my dad has kept me going

throughout my life. As a teacher, real encouragement is being there day to day, being dependable, and standing with students. It is expecting much, but also looking for what is right. I now realize how important a hand on the shoulder, a positive comment on a paper, encouraging cheers at a game, and friendly smiles can be to students. Really, a teacher's influence never stops. When done well, it's the gift that keeps giving.

And I didn't just tell the students. As a teacher I learned firsthand that parents needed to know when their children did something right. So I tried very hard to communicate in writing and in person with families to tell them something positive I had observed their children doing in my class. You certainly get less parental support if the only time you ever communicate is when something is wrong. I'm not being Pollyanna-ish here or suggesting that everyone gets a participation trophy. Affirmations move us when they are given sincerely and specifically.

Students respond to what they are given. Enthusiasm is rewarded with enthusiasm and motivation. Engagement makes it meaningful. Equality promotes opportunity and fairness. Expectations show students how to succeed. Encouragement says you care.

Relationships with Staff and Coworkers

The lessons I learned when building relationships with students gave me a firm foundation to build relationships with teachers, staff members, and colleagues when I moved into leadership roles.

There is nothing quite so invigorating as jumping headfirst into a job you have never had before, when you're not sure what you are supposed to do. I intuitively followed the advice of Dr. Charles Mayo, founder of the world-famous clinic with his name. When asked what advice he would give a beginning medical doctor, he said to imagine that they were a patient.

What kind of doctor would they want? Then be that kind of doctor. That is pretty good advice for any professional in their first assignment.

When I became a principal, I imagined I was a teacher at my school. What kind of principal would I want? Two veteran teachers who had worked with numerous principals put my role in perspective pretty early on with this question: "Are you going to be a princi-PAL or a princi-PILE?" I got the meaning and early on determined to do things with people and not to them.

How do you do things *with* people? Ask questions. Be present and available. Know something. Act. Follow up. Keep your word. Even now with all the technological changes, testing, accountability, etc., these principles still matter.

RAK

I have experienced the reciprocal effect of practicing random acts of kindness in all phases and dimensions of my life. Psychologist William James noted that the deepest human craving is to be appreciated. Dale Carnegie shares a story in his seminal work *How to Win Friends and Influence People* about a lady who asks her husband to list six things that would help her become a better wife. The husband remarked later, "It would have been easy for me to list six things I'd like to change about her. She could have listed a thousand things she would have liked to change about me." He told her he would think about it and give her an answer in the morning. The next morning he got up, called a florist, and sent roses to his wife with a note saying, "I can't think of six things I'd change about you. I love you the way you are."

One of Carnegie's central assertions is to become genuinely interested in others, as he says it, to "put ourselves out to do things for other people— things that require time, energy, unselfishness, and thoughtfulness." Carnegie illustrated these principles using ordinary stories from people who attended his classes. Here's one more.

One man described himself at ten years old, waiting in the welfare ward of the city hospital on Thanksgiving Day to undergo surgery the next morning. His father was deceased, and his mother couldn't visit that day. Overwhelmed with despair and loneliness, he began sobbing. "A young nursing student heard my sobbing and came over to talk to me," he said. "She told me how lonely she was having to work that day and not being able to be with her family. She asked me if I would have dinner with her. She brought turkey, potatoes, and ice cream. And though scheduled to leave at 4:00, she stayed until 11:00 playing games with me until I fell asleep." Such is the power of warmth, genuine care, and interest. Those are the things we remember about others. Carnegie's work illustrates the true adage, "People don't care how much you know until they know how much you care."

People in their eighties and nineties can still fondly remember a positive thing a teacher said to them in second grade—that they had common sense, that they were smart, funny, or a good writer. Sometimes those messages change the direction of a person's life.

As I look back, the most important thing I ever did was writing personal notes to people. It just made sense at the time to thank, acknowledge, and encourage people. I didn't go to thank-you note school, but it goes a long way. Mark Twain was right when he said, "I can last two months on a good compliment." But it wasn't until I read the book *Random Acts of Kindness* that I put a system in place for practicing kindness. The book's premise was really simple—do nice things for people without considering quid pro quo. It's not a version of "I'll scratch your back, you scratch mine." Instead, selfless and anonymous giving is best. Like leaving enough money for the person behind you at Starbucks to get a coffee, or doing the same at a toll booth for the driver behind you. It cultivates goodwill and adds to your general well-being. That is a win-win!

Every Sunday starting with my first year as a principal and continuing today, I make a list of things I need to accomplish in the coming week. Then I cross them off with a highlighter as I complete them so I can see how I'm doing for the week. I must admit that if I don't feel like I'm accomplishing much, I'll place a couple of low hangers on my list that I can quickly do and cross off, giving me a better outlook for my week. But always first on my list are these three letters—RAK—reminding me for over thirty years to do some random acts of kindness. They aren't always anonymous, but a mixed bag of thank-yous, notes to old friends, truly random acts, etc. Since it's first on my list, it is always my priority and it gets done. I think about it, look for opportunities, and yes, feel better about myself when I do it. And it isn't always work related at all.

One winter morning, I had breakfast at a Bob Evans restaurant. When I went to my car, the person next to me had parked too close for me to open the driver's side door. I could get in through the passenger door but didn't think I could crawl over the tight bucket seats and gear shift. I walked back into the restaurant clearly irritated and asked the hostess for help to identify who had parked next to me. The hostess, probably in her fifties with a broad smile, asked, "Can you show me so I know which car is next to you?"

"Of course," I said. "I want you to see what this person did."

She took a look and said she could get in on the passenger side and crawl over, start the car, and back out.

"Are you sure? It's really tight in there."

"Yes," she laughed, "and I want to try."

Of course, my mood had just improved with her enthusiasm, laughter, and countenance. "Okay, here you go," I said as I opened the door and she squeezed into the car. And there she went. Climbing over the console and gear shift and into the driver's seat, she backed right out. I was amazed; I'm fairly fit and I know I couldn't have done what she did. And she did it willingly and happily. She made my day! I went back to the restaurant a couple days later and got her name. I wrote her a beautiful thank-you letter and copied her manager and corporate headquarters. I don't remember her name, but I hope my letter made her day as much as she made mine that cold, snowy winter day.

There is nothing to make you like other human beings so much as doing things for them.
ZORA NEALE HURSTON

THE MAHONEY THREE

ONE: Place RAK (random acts of kindness) on your to-do list each week. Start with one a week, a month, or a quarter. Simply do something un-expected to help, acknowledge, or surprise someone with generosity. The amount of money or effort expended is not as important as the fact that you do it. It might be paying for the person in line behind you at Starbucks or the toll booth. Make a donation, send a card, or surprise an old friend with a text. It may or may not be anonymous, but practicing this type of gratitude will make you more optimistic, healthy, and likely happy. Nothing boosts the spirit more than doing something good for someone else.

TWO: Make a scrapbook of letters for your team or a special group you work with like coaches, music teachers, or development directors. Simply call someone close to each person on that team and ask them to write a letter remembering something special about them or a way they may have helped them. Encourage them to ask others to write a similar letter and return it to you. Collect them all in a scrapbook to present to the person. Once you start, the activity builds upon itself, and more letters will arrive. The scrapbook is a permanent reminder of relationships they've built and how they are making a difference. It says their work and self matters.

THREE: Conclude each staff meeting with public recognition from peers. Give awards a symbolic name so they are associated with praise. At Battelle for Kids, we called ours Valerie Anns after our fictional training character. Create a card people can use to acknowledge others' efforts in writing. At the end of the staff meeting, ask a couple people to come up and read them aloud to everyone. It helps create a culture of recognition and affirmation.

Chapter 16

BUILD CONSTRUCTIVE RELATIONSHIPS

You can make more friends in two months by becoming
interested in other people than you can in two years by
trying to get other people interested in you.
DALE CARNEGIE

LESSONS I LEARNED from building relationships with students apply in all phases of life. In teaching, the better the relationships, the easier and more enjoyable the job is, and the more students will learn. In business, the better relationships you have with coworkers, the more enjoyable and productive the work is.

PIES

Bringing Out the Best in Teachers provides some salient research on how to build constructive relationships. I made up an acronym to help me remember the main ideas: PIES, which stands for praise, involvement, expectations, and "standing beside."

PRAISE AND RESPECT

You can build relationships with and among staff by establishing a tradition of authentic praise and respect. Teachers and most employees crave feedback and get so little of it. Suppose we led a scavenger hunt with people over fifty, and I asked them to find a written note from a student, parent, colleague, or administrator that praised, affirmed, or complimented them in some way. How many could bring a note back? All of them. Why? Because notes matter even more than money.

As a first-year teacher, I coached junior high basketball. At the start of the season our superintendent gave me an eagle patch (our team mascot) with a short note wishing me luck. It was sincere, unexpected, and most certainly appreciated. The fact that I remember this forty-five years later is testimony to its staying power. Years later, as superintendent, I sent a little district pin to each new teacher six weeks after school had started with a note sharing a positive thought from their principal and telling them I was happy they had chosen to work in our district. I didn't do it with the intent to manipulate them later; it was simply a sincere effort to encourage the people who do the real work in schools each day.

Just as I had sent notes home as a teacher about positive things students did, I made a habit of regularly handwriting small notes of appreciation, encouragement, or affirmation to staff members. I didn't assign criteria to it and didn't care if they received accolades from others for the same thing. I did it because it felt right. Of all the things a leader can do, none is as important or as simple as giving recognition for a job well done. Tell people in writing. They will keep the notes forever, and each time they read them they will relive the experience over again.

At my first staff meeting as a new principal, I announced that I wanted teachers to send two notes home each night with students who had done things right or moved in the right direction, just as I had done as a teacher, just to let their parents know. I was clear about what I expected—two notes each day to students of their choosing for whatever they wanted to affirm.

But what you expect, you need to inspect. Ten minutes before the end of school the day after I set the expectation, I walked in a classroom unannounced and asked a teacher which students she had written notes to that day. I didn't just pick a random teacher, but one I knew was an opinion leader in the building. She could only have given one of two responses: either she'd written her notes to students A and B or she hadn't. I suspected the latter.

She stammered, completely surprised. I quickly acknowledged that she was probably getting ready to write the notes, and I would take the class for the last ten minutes so she could. I did, she did, and then we talked after school about the students she chose. I thanked her, then counted on one more thing happening, though I have no evidence it did. I hoped she would tell everyone in the teacher's lounge the next day what I had done.

I checked in with the teacher before the end of the day to avoid a "gotcha" moment and the inevitable confrontation. I wanted her to do it and then tell others. Expect first and inspect next. And lastly: respect. How do you as the leader show respect for others in your expectations for them? In this case, I wrote notes to teachers. Show them you believe in and practice what you are asking them to do. It is really leadership 101: don't expect of others what you don't expect of yourself.

Rarely have I met a leader operating at their best who didn't care about their people and want them to feel appreciated. But few go beyond thinking about it to intentionally doing it. Recognition is strategic. Organizations ought to plan for staff recognition and appreciation as conscientiously as they prepare their annual budget. You wouldn't leave that to chance. Be committed to catching people doing right! And make it special for them. A few special moments in someone's life can have enormous impact. Rarely can you invest so little and have so much returned for your organization.

I loved going back to the office on the day before Valentine's Day to place wrapped flowers on staff members' desks, having them wonder who the flower fairy was. On Mother's Day, I'd place a beautiful basket of flowers on a mother's desk with a card thanking her and asking that she pass the flowers on to another mother in the office to enjoy after thirty minutes.

Don Clifton and his grandson Tom Rath captured this notion perfectly in their bestselling book *How Full Is Your Bucket?*, which clearly demonstrates that the more positivity we provide, the more we acquire. Our metaphorical bucket is emptied or filled by what others say or do to us. But when we use our dippers to fill others' buckets, it replenishes ours as well.

Can praise be overdone? Of course, and nothing is more disingenuous than a sugary sweet person who overdoes the verbal praise and then treats people miserably, or lets their exuberance lead to purchases they can't afford or deals they shouldn't make. But a healthy dose of optimism matters!

You might create a tradition like we did at Battelle for Kids with "Valerie Anns." Valerie Ann was a mythical figure that we used in value-added training. Our graphic designer gave her an identity. We made up little cards to say something nice about someone else and finished every staff meeting by reading a handful of them aloud. Authors were anonymous. Our enterprising and creative COO often added interesting wrinkles. For example, the entire staff might get a note from him that said Valerie Ann wanted three words to thank a colleague. In February he might ask staff to show some love for Valentine's Day, and drop a line to thank a colleague for something they did in the last month to move the team forward. Thus we always ended our staff meetings with powerful, positive comments from staff.

I can't tell you how many people over the years appreciated hearing these comments. These were written by staff for staff, authentically; if you listened to just a year's worth of these notes, you had a feel for who was contributing in ways the staff felt was worthy, and how. These notes were often humorous, always sincere, and they contributed to the culture of appreciation that we wanted. Well-planned staff meetings were an important device we used regularly to promote them.

Affirmation matters. Ask Oprah: in her Harvard commencement address she said that the thousands of people she interviewed, from past presidents to miscreants, all wanted to know the same thing. After the cameras stopped rolling they looked at her and said, "Was that okay?" We need affirmation and feedback. During the Korean War, North Korean POWs died at a much higher rate because those held in prison were denied all forms of human contact, especially affirmation in the form of letters and calls from home. All was denied, proving that total lack of affirmation was the worst kind of punishment. It was psychologist William James who noted the deepest principle in human craving is to be appreciated.

But remember my essential point. Find ways to thank and honor the people you interact with. Do it regularly. Plan for it. Make it authentic. Inauthentic affirmation is just ass-kissing, and the fact that it works reveals how thirsty we all are for affirmation—even when it comes with cynicism or outright dishonesty. Most of all, practice affirmation for your staff. Find ways to appreciate, reward, understand, and acknowledge people.

One of the most beautiful compensations of life is that you cannot give a bouquet of flowers to someone else without retaining some of the fragrance for yourself.
RALPH WALDO EMERSON

INVOLVEMENT AND ENGAGEMENT

Involvement in meaningful projects is engaging for everyone. If you want people in the game, cut them in on the deal. The trick is deciding which issues to involve them in. My graduate education came in handy here, and I used a theory I learned in my coursework. It works.

A leading researcher in organizational psychology, Fred Fiedler, suggested using a four-quadrant grid to discern whether to involve staff in a particular decision. On one dimension he plotted the importance of the outcome to the staff; on the other he plotted staff expertise in the decision-making area. Where the outcome is important and staff expertise is high, Fiedler argues, always include staff in the decision-making process. Where they are both low, don't waste their time.

For example, schedules matter to teachers because that is where real priorities show up. Let them wrestle with the principals to influence the schedule. On the other hand, I remember being part of a staff meeting as a teacher where we spent the entire time debating whether kids should be allowed to chew gum. Nobody had expertise in this area, just opinions, and it didn't really matter that much. In those instances, the leader needs to make a decision and move on. Also, the principal needs to clearly communicate that including people does not mean totally ceding authority to them. Hell hath no fury like a committee scorned! But teachers want to be part of the process, and if you don't include them you miss out on their expertise and, worse yet, their followership and participation.

Participation: There is no better word to describe what good teachers and leaders do to produce results. Can you think of a time when you were really applying a skill by remaining passive? That is not to say there is never a time for active listening. But if you keep people there, you lose them. Lecture is a great way to learn, but it can't go on forever (nor is it a preferred method when the lecturer is a poor speaker).

Staff members at any organization want to share their expertise, knowledge, and experience. Employers want commitment. The two go hand in hand. The Gallup Organization's Q12 survey, which is given in thousands of organizations, clearly documents the relationship between employee engagement and organizational performance. The more affirmatively people answer the twelve questions, the higher performance is more likely to be. So why don't more leaders employ such strategies to measure staff engagement? If I said you will have more rewards for everyone if you do X, Y, and Z, wouldn't you do it? Especially if it wasn't something difficult to perform. The Q12 can be taken online quite simply and at low cost. The questions reveal things you can act on inexpensively. I can only guess that sometimes organizations don't act because of a sense of arrogance, an attitude that says "I know best," "I'm the best," and "I'm in charge." Sometimes it comes from not knowing *how* to engage people. Others may view it as a waste of time.

Engagement is not about sharing ignorance, screaming opinions at each other, or allowing thoughtless people to prescribe actions they have no responsibility to implement. But if leaders act with the belief that none of us is as smart as all of us, engagement can be a productive step to ultimate success. In *The Wisdom of Crowds*, James Surowiecki presents clear evidence that informed, regular people often make better decisions than the experts who are often encumbered by too much knowledge or false certainty from their experience and credentials.

Over the years I have served as a consultant to several boards searching for their next CEO. This is an opportunity to engage staff, clients, and other relevant partners in a discussion. At a minimum, you can figure out what is on people's minds and capture ideas to propel performance for the next leader. Rarely does it make sense, even in good times, to believe that we need someone just like the last person, even if they were very successful. I always started by suggesting how the board might engage others.

On one occasion, I consulted with a school board that was adamant that they alone should choose the next superintendent. Of course it was their duty. But they believed asking others for their opinion was a dereliction of that duty. One board member perfectly summarized the sentiment of the entire board by declaring, "This is why we are elected." Others don't say it, but sometimes what they mean is, "We know who we want."

Another time a board president expressed the same sentiment after fully reviewing numerous options to include others in the planning process. "We don't need them. It's a waste of time. We were elected to do this." And so it goes. Who really believes that alienating your workforce, citizens, and clients is an especially good strategy for improved performance? That doesn't mean that those who don't engage others can't get it right. They do sometimes. But when you include others in the process, you increase your probability of success. Commitment usually follows engagement, and engagement precedes production. Like most things in life, it's pretty easy to describe but hard to do.

The same principle applies to efforts to raise taxes to finance new buildings or programs. Include the community in the deal. There is abundant evidence that citizen engagement increases the likelihood that a levy will pass. Why wouldn't a school board or superintendent do that? For some of the same reasons I mentioned earlier. Or the fact that collaboration is messy, uneven, and sometimes distracting. But it works if it is thoughtfully approached, communicated using accurate information, and successfully led.

As a superintendent, my school district faced the dual challenges of higher costs (largely due to health insurance) and student overcrowding. We brought together nearly two hundred citizens in the community to hear the facts, wrestle in table groups with what the board was considering, and share their discussion table by table. Several people cautioned me against such an approach. "What will you do if the groups suggest mixed approaches? What if some say to pass an operations levy first and solve the facilities issue later, and others say just the opposite? Or reduce expenditures by reducing board contributions to health insurance? Or lay off staff and increase class sizes?" The thinking was that this type of dialogue makes you look indecisive and encourages confusion, not leadership.

I responded, "If we don't facilitate this conversation with the community, do you think that people won't share their ideas about it?" They'd share them all right—in the parking lot meeting, which happens after the official meeting. Inside, people are polite, never talk about the elephant in the room, and, in the interest of loyalty or civility, never bring up what they really think. The real opinions are expressed after the meeting, outside in the parking lot. I wanted to bring the parking lot meeting inside.

Still, some suggested, if you are going to have twenty-five tables, appoint a leader at each table to guide the discussion the way you want it to go.

"No," I said. "That looks like manipulation, and these are smart people. I don't know the best answer to this challenge, nor does the board. But I appreciate and respect that they trust the community enough to ask them—to *engage* them." And so, after weeks of planning to have the right information on hand, develop the right questions, and frame the challenge to the community properly, we held our three-hour Saturday meeting.

This particular session included officers of every school group, from music and sports boosters at the high school to PTO leaders at the elementary schools. Business leaders, local government leaders, and opinion leaders from across the community were encouraged to attend. The group was not selected to breed harmony, but rather to provide real diversity of viewpoints and perspectives. Did I second guess having the meeting, especially after naysayers called it a punt, a lack of leadership? Yes.

The night before our gathering, I was extremely nervous. But I thought of Abe Lincoln's quote, and began the group session by reciting it. "Without public sentiment, nothing can succeed. With it, nothing can fail." We needed the community engaged in thinking about this challenge. After all, it was their money we might ultimately be asking for. A levy is a poor way to gauge community support without engaging them first, especially if you had multiple options.

What happened next solidified for me forever the power of public engagement. The surprise? Nearly every table suggested an approach the board had never really considered: two new levies at the same time—a facilities levy and an operations levy. It was clear to me after the meeting that our approach should be exactly that. We held several more meetings to give others the chance to weigh in, but the die was cast after this first meeting. These opinion leaders talked to folks across the community, and several weeks later the school board voted unanimously to place two new four-mill levies on the ballot—one for facility improvement and another for operations. And while we revved up the levy campaign over the next three months, the result was really guaranteed in that large community meeting. It was there that they said yes to our challenge, there that they offered solutions to consider, and there that they had been brought into the conversation and empowered to help solve the problem.

The result? My happiest day ever as superintendent. Both issues passed with nearly 60 percent approval. Back then we assigned people to physically collect poll results from all precincts and bring them back to our centralized middle school where we could count them more quickly than the official count, which occurred later in the county seat. I was posted at a precinct where no issue had ever passed. The grumpy lady in charge knew who I was. I waited impatiently for her to post the results. When she walked out, she looked warily at me and barked, "Well, you lost both issues." It was true. We had lost, but by only three votes in one case and four in the other, in a precinct that historically defeated school issues by a wide margin. When I saw those results I grinned at her and said, "Thank you. I'm pretty certain we just won." I headed back to my car to join the others.

Do I think you'll win every time you engage a community in a taxing situation? Of course not. But public leadership is about engagement. When you engage others, you ask, listen, influence, consider, and lead. If you want real support from others, it usually begins with this powerful, inviting question or some variation of it: "What do you think?"

I was running early one morning in a neighborhood where several houses and apartments were being constructed. I could hear numerous carpenters hammering nails as they framed the structures. It produced a kind of cacophony, a symphony if you will, that to me sounded beautiful. You hear, of course, what you listen for. On that morning this sound was a symphony of many people working individually, but in concert and in service to something bigger than themselves. That's what engagement does.

EXPECTATIONS

We talked about expectations in Chapter 15, but it bears repeating here. Robust research shows that teacher expectations accelerate student achievement, and this is equally true for all relationships. As a principal, what do you expect of staff members? How do you communicate those expectations? Oftentimes when teaching graduate classes in administration to teachers, I would pretend I was a news reporter, asking each person to outline their principal's expectations: what they stood for, what they wouldn't allow, or what they insisted upon. Answers varied from the perfunctory (be to school on time) to the philosophical (provide equality of opportunity). What always surprised me was the large number of people who simply couldn't answer the question. They didn't know what their principal believed, expected, or valued.

Employees are motivated by clear expectations even if they don't agree with them. This isn't about micromanaging but about communication culture. Let staff know the values you stand for and how you expect them to uphold those values. Let's say you believe literacy is the most important skill students can learn. You know that silent sustained reading each day will promote that value, so you read your own book to model it and provide the uninterrupted time each day for everyone to do it with their students. Or maybe it's as simple as being to school on time early each day, greeting kids as they get off the bus, or dressing professionally. You need to model what you expect, or the expectation falls flat.

Remember that expectations must come with support. Provide support, opportunities to practice, and feedback to improve. Model the behaviors and practice what you preach. Don't expect of others what you don't expect of yourself. As the leader, you go first. And lastly, remember to expect first and inspect next: follow up to make sure your expectations are implemented.

STANDING BESIDE

"Standing beside" means being present with the staff as a leader, especially in difficult times. If you know a teacher has a challenging parent conference, "standing beside" is offering to be present if they need you. One of the best and worst examples of this both happened to me on the same morning. I was teaching at the elementary school and coaching spring softball at the high school. I got a call late on a school night that two players had been involved in a fist fight involving alcohol. Parents were mad, and I said we would all meet at 8:00 the next morning at the high school to sort it out.

Early the next day I called my principal to ask if someone could cover my morning class at the elementary school while I sorted through the mess with my players at the high school. He said yes. Then I called the high school principal to inform him that I'd be there with several students and mad parents. He told me he had to go to a county principals' meeting that morning and that he would affirm whatever I decided to do in terms of discipline. He even said there were suspension papers in his top drawer. Let me stop here.

Suspension papers in the top drawer? I had no clue how to suspend a student. This small, rural high school had no assistant principal, so I was on my own. I said okay, but even now I can feel my total unease at the prospect of unwinding a conflict and taking the appropriate steps. I had very little experience with any of this, but I started the meeting determined to simply be fair and worry about procedure later. There was *no one* standing beside or even near me.

Just after the meeting started, though, the principal came in, took control of the meeting, and handled it deftly. After it was all over, he told me that while he was driving to his meeting he realized I probably needed his help more than the county principals did. He turned his car around and came back to the high school. He was right. I learned a lot that day, but what I remember most is how he stood beside me. Do you think I became a supporter for him? Only forever. That is standing beside.

Evaluations

I've taken to asking people to describe themselves in three words. There's a mystique of three in communication. It's just the right number. Look around and you will see three words everywhere: on medical centers, colleges, businesses, books (think *Eat, Pray, Love*), and even pizza trucks. (One I saw said "Order. Pay. Leave.") You get the idea. Three verbs are memorable, concise, and actionable.

One year I was asked to deliver a keynote address to teachers at their district convocation. I decided to do a little pre-work and call teachers I knew, asking them what three verbs they would choose to be evaluated by.

I said, "Think of verbs you would want your work to be judged by and what evidence you would present to verify that judgment." The latter is important because if your actions don't reflect your beliefs, it doesn't mean much. If you choose the word *welcome* because you want each child to feel appreciated, invited, and encouraged in your room, you had better not appear to be anything to the contrary. That doesn't work.

This exercise also causes people to think about the purpose and intended outcomes of their work. It can be used by any professional. Frankly, if I were the education czar, I'd throw out all the checklists, rubrics, and complicated processes in favor of this simple exercise aimed at promoting discussion and getting at the heart of what someone does, why they do it, and what evidence they can provide to back up their results. But I digress.

The first teacher I called gave the words *prepare, observe, learn*. The next one said *encourage, support, motivate*. Another: *align, assess, achieve*. Then the exercise that began as a way to prepare a speech became a game for me. How many teachers would I need to call before a verb was repeated? It turns out seven. I collected twenty different verbs from teachers before one was repeated. I had an "aha" moment: *You do your job the way you see and think about your job.*

This simple exercise encourages profound conversations with teachers. Just ask, "What are your three verbs?" You could do this prospectively for new hires or even retrospectively, asking for evidence to back up their answers. While I never consciously used this framework as a principal or superintendent, I can look back on my body of work and answer clearly. What were my three verbs? *Engage, improve, cultivate.* There are certainly others, but these are *my* three, not the right three. The beauty of this exercise is that it encourages discussion, reflection, and action.

Mentor Relationships

Perhaps nothing defines and improves a leader more than who they emulate and learn from. Mentors provide those "fire with iron" moments that turn to steel. In 1971, Swen Nater was the junior college basketball player of the year. He wanted to play Division I basketball for the best coach and team in America. That part was easy: Coach John Wooden and his UCLA Bruins had won many championships in a row, and that is exactly who Swen wanted to play center for the next year. The problem was that UCLA had a center named Bill Walton who would be starting for the next three years. Coach Wooden told Swen that he would probably never start a game if he came to UCLA, but he could start, play, and be a star at many other schools.

Swen persisted, and eventually Coach Wooden took him. What happened? Swen never started a game. But he played against the best players in the country every night in practice and made himself and them better. When Swen left UCLA, he took with him three National Championship rings. And what else? It was the first time that a player who had never started a game became a first-round draft choice for the NBA. He went on to have a very successful NBA career. That's the value of association. Align yourself with those from whom you can learn effectively and be humble enough to listen to them, seek their advice, and ask for help when you need it.

I've been fortunate to have excellent mentors in my career. One was Larry Miller, a district superintendent who had already served fifteen years in his role at this time. We were totally different back then. He was the businessman superintendent—well-dressed, supremely confident but never cocky, quiet but highly competitive, with incredible business acumen and financial skills. I was his "not"—not well-dressed, not business oriented, not quiet, not reserved. Yet he knew the district, especially teachers, needed a guide on the ground, someone who would listen, act, and work with them to improve student experience. My selection alone is testimony to his confidence, loyalty to his organization, and ability to see what it needed. Although we were very different, he knew that I would share his goals for the district: more student opportunities, higher student performance, more effective teachers, more operational efficiencies, and a great reputation. He was the first person I met who really believed in working with people and behaved accordingly. He believed the key to realizing his dreams for students was an empowered, talented, and hard-working staff.

Operations was his biggest strength. He knew how to budget, buy buses at the right time, manage food service and all the rest, increasing efficiency so more dollars could be redirected to student programming. He wanted me to work the other side of the house—curriculum, student programming, and instruction. I was blessed to have someone who knew how to constructively corral my exuberance, encourage my risk taking, and support my learning. He was the one who stood by me after my disastrous in-service experience and told me, "Remember that there are no failures, just lessons."

Another of my mentors was Dr. Bill Sanders, whom I recruited to work with me at Battelle for Kids. It could be reasonably argued that Bill was one of the most influential education reformers of the late twentieth and early twenty-first centuries. He was recognized by several national organizations shortly before his death in 2017. No one person influenced or taught me more in this chapter of my life than Bill.

Who you hook your wagon up to matters, and in Bill I found the absolute right person at the right time to propel the work of Battelle for Kids. He was brilliant, and I don't say that lightly. As he used to say (and never about himself) when someone could communicate effectively, "He can get the hay to the ponies!" While he was never a schoolteacher, Bill was a world-class statistician and teacher par excellence. He had a unique ability to take something technical and complicated—value-added methodology—and make it easier to understand without oversimplifying it. He most wanted to improve public education and provide teachers, principals, and superintendents with information to improve their decision making. He was authentic, never wavering from his commitment to help educators understand the data and increase opportunities for children. When he spoke, he oozed sincerity and credibility. I love this quote from him in response to a superintendent's question about data and truth: "I know you can lie with numbers. But as a statistician, I also know it's easier to lie without numbers."

Mentors come in all shapes and sizes. In addition to having great personal mentors, I also had the opportunity through my dissertation to study a dozen great superintendents in Ohio. I learned how they managed teams, handled conflict, passed levies, worked effectively with boards, and implemented successful change. Not that I could have (or should have) done it exactly their way. But I learned methods that were skillful, helpful, and instructive to me. Find these people. Learn from them.

One of the things we did at Battelle for Kids was to adopt the Appreciative Inquiry approach to organizational change developed by David Cooperrider, which focuses on an organization's strengths (instead of its weaknesses) as the basis of change. Our study, *The Best Teacher in You*, looked at the work of teachers who were making spectacular academic gains with kids to figure out what they were doing right. Appreciative Inquiry is about finding and building on what is right about something. We used the same approach to study effective leadership building.

Though I didn't know it, I practiced this method in my early years of teaching by visiting successful classrooms in other schools, watching athletic practices of successful coaches, and visiting superintendents when I did my dissertation. I never had anyone turn me down. When you ask to learn from someone who is doing something right, how do you think they feel about it? Conversations go like this: "We have reviewed data from your classroom/

building and the results over time are remarkable. There is zero chance this happened randomly. We would like to visit, learn from you, and then share our results—attributing you, of course. Is that possible?"

The answer is almost always yes. This is Appreciative Inquiry.

Can you learn from those who do something poorly? Absolutely. But while I never have asked, the conversation about visiting these places might be a little awkward at best! Cooperrider advises, "Merciless criticism often makes us dig in our heels in defense, or worse, makes us helpless." This is not about failing to address weaknesses but beginning with strengths. Start with what is right.

The relationships I have developed and maintained throughout my life have been critical to any success I have had. Whether they be students, employees, colleagues, or board members, I know that engaging people, communicating expectations, involving them in projects and decisions, treating them fairly and with respect, encouraging them, learning from them, and affirming their value are the keys to the most rewarding experiences.

THE MAHONEY THREE

ONE: Pretend an evaluator is asking you to choose three verbs that characterize your prioritized goals for the upcoming year. What are your three? Explain to a partner why you chose those three and what evidence you would provide to show that you accomplished them. Listing your three verbs alone or with a group helps you determine what work is most important and how it aligns to actions and results. It also reveals your beliefs and leadership style.

TWO: Measure staff engagement. Now. Use Gallup's long-running Q12 survey (at Gallup.com), which asks staff to respond to twelve questions on a Likert scale. Positive responses indicate higher engagement. Gallup's research suggests engagement is a proxy for impact, higher profitability, more worker satisfaction, less absenteeism, etc. Get a baseline now and work on areas with the lowest scores. Figure out what you are doing right in areas with high scores and continue being intentional in those actions. Remeasure periodically to determine if you are moving the dial and improving outcomes for the organization.

THREE: Make a two-by-two grid (Fiedler model) for considering staff input on decision-making, with staff expertise on one axis and importance of the outcome to the organization on the other. Think about decisions coming up in the near and long term, and put each issue in the proper quadrant based upon these factors. Where staff has expertise and the decision is important, consider how best to involve staff to improve engagement and, likely, the results. In the quadrant where staff expertise is low and the decision is relatively unimportant, don't waste their time.

Chapter 17

BUILD PRODUCTIVE RELATIONSHIPS WITH BOARDS

The greatest compliment ever paid to me was when someone asked me what I thought, and attended to my answer.
HENRY DAVID THOREAU

THIS CHAPTER MIGHT BE most interesting to people who have to work with a school board or board of directors. The lessons I learned from teaching apply here as well. A school board or corporate board of directors is a group of people responsible for governing an organization. A board is responsible to its stakeholders, who might be stockholders or the citizens of a community. Sometimes the goals of the board are compatible with the goals of the organization's leaders and employees, and sometimes they are not.

One of the things I've learned over the years is a paradox of leadership: what you like is also what you don't like. You may like working on something, but you also don't like it. It can be that way with boards. I enjoyed working with boards, but on occasion I didn't like working with them (or at least an individual member or two). A good relationship with your board fosters accountability, motivation to get things done, and support for difficult decisions. Board relationships and how successfully you work with them make all the difference.

When I was thirty-eight, the school board was considering a second contract for me after three years as their superintendent. When they completed their review I announced, "Look at it this way. You are getting the enthusiasm of youth coupled with the look of maturity." With my receding hairline, I certainly looked older than my age. One member grinned and said, "You are so full of it." Then, hesitating slightly, he added, "But I'm going to vote for it!"

While I never worked *for* boards, I clearly understood that I worked at their pleasure. I don't mean that I got up in the morning and thought, *What am I going to do today that will make the board happy?* Nor, fortunately, did a board ever expect me to cater to individual whims. I worked fifteen years for boards of education and another fifteen years for a not-for-profit board with very different members and expectations. So, my stories come from experience, watching many other CEO-board relationships up close, and mining ideas from the research on successful executive board relations. This includes finding the right fit, keeping communication lines open, and recognizing shared purpose.

Fit

Successful board relationships begin by finding the right fit. I conducted numerous superintendent searches over the years and could usually predict which candidate was going to be offered the job. A colleague once shared a telltale sign, and he was right: you could tell who was a good fit when the interview turned into a natural conversation. Board members began by asking scripted questions such as, "What would you do to get to know our community?" And the candidate would respond more or less formally. "I'd meet with parent group leaders, the mayor's office, and faith-based heads, then I'd broaden my search to meet with as many people as possible." This continued until, in some cases, a kind of chemistry broke out. Instead of stopping with the formal answer, the candidate might look at all the members and sincerely ask, "Who do you think I should meet with to best get to know the community?" One board member, unscripted, might answer, "You have got to talk to Mr. Hodge, our local funeral director. He's been here for years, knows everybody, likes to help, and would offer good ideas." Another might add, "Don't forget Cecelia Parks. She was a longtime principal, volunteers throughout the community, and is widely respected by folks around here." You can see the difference, and when you are there, you feel it too.

Why is this so important? Because connection matters. The board and candidate connected and began a conversation because it came easily and naturally. Sure, it often begins with a question from the candidate, but the member wanted to answer it and the candidate asked more questions. Pretty soon people were really getting to know each other and, better yet, like each other. Likability is a two-way street and real connection takes both sides. I often cautioned boards that if they hoped to get the best person, that person had to want the board and the organization too. They were not simply hired help, nor did they want to feel that way. Fit, of course, is not determined by a single interview any more than mates are determined by two-minute speed dating, but you can get an initial feel.

Fit is largely determined by context. What does the organization need going forward to be successful? That's influenced by many things, especially the behavior of the last CEO. Let's be honest here. Leaders can do anything; they just can't do everything. And our strengths are strengths until they are not. Let's say the last CEO was a person who would always listen to ideas and challenges and offer support. People loved the fact that they could pop in almost any time for a conversation. The CEO was always patient, interminably thoughtful, and never reactive. Sounds good, doesn't it? Until you need a decision, energy to execute a plan, and occasionally outrage. Nope. Not in this person's DNA. That's why I support organizational leadership change, especially in a public setting. Leaders don't get to stay forever. They are guardians. And the best leaders know when it's time to leave.

Dr. Frank Walters, longtime state superintendent of Ohio, liked to tell the story of a local superintendent who came to him after a contentious board meeting. An altercation had taken place, and he was worried that he might lose his license.

"What happened?" Frank asked.

"The guy [a board member] is always questioning my integrity and disputing everything we decide to do, and we were all fed up with him, especially me."

Frank queried further, "What did you do?"

"I lost my cool, went over and punched him in the mouth. I realized instantly I had made a mistake and left the board meeting."

Frank couldn't promise the superintendent that his certificate would not be pulled, as it depended on whether charges were filed. As it turned out, the superintendent was charged with a misdemeanor and paid a seventy-dollar fine. He called Frank afterward to thank him for listening and to add an epilogue to the story. The day after he paid the fine, he found an envelope on his desk at work. It contained seventy dollars and a small note that simply said, "Hit him again."

Sometimes, without placing blame, the fit isn't right. The point is that your strengths, interests, and skills need to match the needs of the organization to ensure a higher probability of success. That's why third-party search consultants can be invaluable to the process. They can formally and informally assess candidates' strengths and properly analyze the situation through interviews and other tools. Fit is partly determined by patterns of natural behavior.

For example, I asked final candidates for one job to give me twenty-five references. Their initial reaction was, "What?!" They probably thought I was crazy, as did board members when I assigned them to call five references each. My rationale was simple. This selection process was no longer about references really. Candidates had long passed that bar. They were experienced, successful, knowledgeable, and all the rest. It was now about fit.

Many questions were written to elicit behavioral responses, not judgment. Board members weren't asking references whether the candidate was a good person, but questions that prompted a discussion of behavior—how will the candidate act and react in a given situation? Is that the behavior that will work best in this setting? It was an attempt to evaluate fit. Does this person have the right temperament, behavior, skills, and experience to do what you need them to do? If the district needs someone who connects with the community, makes allies easily, enjoys getting out to meet people—can this candidate do that? The road is littered with high-profile leaders in all sectors who were simply the wrong fit because the board had not considered what kind of leader they needed. A good beginning often determines the ending. Does it ensure it? Nope. The selection process, especially for leaders, is sometimes more art than science.

Communication

So, you have the job. You have a board. How do you make it work for you and the organization? You can easily find articles and textbooks that suggest lists of things the board and superintendent should do. In the '80s a consultant introduced me to the mysterious "green line," a metaphor to describe how one side infringes on the other side. It was important to not cross the green line. It reminds me of the caution I and hundreds of teachers were given when we began our teaching careers: "Don't smile until Christmas."

Well, my experience after all these years has been this: Those who don't smile before Christmas rarely smile after it! Like all sage advice, it's rooted in a degree of truth. Do clear expectations and role responsibilities between the board and superintendent need to be clarified for success? Yes. Do beginning teachers need to determine classroom expectations for students' behavior? Absolutely. It just isn't as clear cut as a green line or a smile.

How do you start? With a conversation. It's what works for the board and you. A new superintendent might ask, "How often do you want to communicate and about what?" or, "How do you want the annual budget developed and presented?" The list is endless; pick the items most important to you and them. What matters here is that you agree and feel comfortable with the approaches you choose. That is what makes it work. Some superintendents would rather make a quick call to board members than trade countless memos. For others it's just the opposite. Have this conversation as a group. Get to know people, because this relationship has a huge impact on the organization's culture. I like how one successful longtime superintendent explained it to me. "We agreed that the board did the defining and I did the doing. We unpacked what that meant, and I worked like hell to implement things well on their behalf."

The board's most important role is to select a superintendent, who in turn needs to figure out how best to work with these (usually elected) community members to make good things happen for children. The time you spend up front deciding, clarifying, and understanding how to operate together will save time and heartache later. As a construction manager said to me during a large-scale building project, "Why is there never enough money to do something right in the first place, but always enough to do it over after it's been screwed up?"

As a county superintendent, I helped create a new education service center with a voluntary merger of three counties (motivated by financial incentives from the state, a desire to increase the collective voice of our small rural districts, and potential savings from collaboration). Condensing three elected boards into one, consolidating personnel with different salaries for the same jobs, and continuing to serve each district were just part of this puzzle. Again, transparency, listening, and building trust were indispensable.

I felt like a shuttle diplomat as I met with boards independently to discuss advantages, concerns, and ideas, building trust person by person by honestly and sincerely listening, clarifying points, and resolving challenges. I worried that putting these groups together before they'd built trust in each other would result in too many unsaid concerns. But they trusted me, and we came to full agreement gradually. Each board met separately to adopt a set of "intentions," because only the new board would have authority to implement the new policies. When all three boards met together for the first time, they had already separately agreed to a new seven-member board (reduced from fifteen members over time), a common salary schedule, and new service delivery plans. I'm happy to say, twenty years later, the foundation we laid prospered and expanded during a time when 70 to 90 percent of all mergers and acquisitions were failing, according to *Harvard Business Review*.

Shared Purpose

Different types of boards operate differently, and each has its value. I was especially blessed at Battelle for Kids to have a governing board that was extraordinarily accomplished. During my fifteen-year tenure, its members included two former CEOs and other senior staff from Battelle Memorial Institute, two former Ohio governors, and presidents of commercial enterprises like insurance companies and banks. How different were they from the farmers, small business folks, and involved parents who served as governing board members when I was superintendent? Let's start with the biggest similarity: people are people. They want to be in regular communication, engaged in appropriate ways, and part of a successful organization. They want their time, energy, and expertise used wisely.

But how I engaged each board was quite different because our goals were different. In schools we planned the budget; at Battelle for Kids we budgeted the plan. In the former, budgets are more regulated and mandated, including what programs to offer, class sizes, and funding for academics or transportation. Everything is subject to rules, laws, contracts, and the like, leaving little room for creativity, real autonomy, or thinking outside the proverbial box. At Battelle for Kids our goal was to sustain ourselves financially, and that accounting was very black and white. In our early years, much emphasis was placed on the numbers. We had to be careful or the board might intervene by reviewing financials, or worse yet, prescribing solutions without really understanding the business enterprise.

Part of my role at Battelle for Kids was to help board members understand our work without making them technical experts. I needed to cultivate just enough understanding so they could provide marketing expertise, offer political advice (to support a proposed law that would help clients), or suggest criteria to consider in a new potential partnership. Our meetings were more focused, business-like, and constructive, because our operating world was different from school boards. While capitalism has a destructive side, its rewards, accounting, and relationship to your work are crystal clear. I explained it this way to the board at Battelle for Kids: "You are all successful leaders. But imagine at your next board meeting you have a thousand guests, so you have moved it to an auditorium. All of those thousand guests have every stick of information that you as board members have in front of you. I promise you it changes the decision-making calculus."

There is a world of difference between leading elected board members in a public setting and selected board members with expertise in a private setting. Business boards have advantages schools could only wish for. Let's start with transparency. Transparency can create trust, but there are times when it thwarts it. In business, managers can reward employees monetarily commensurate with their performance. That's done privately. If a private enterprise listed bonuses on their website for all to see, they would invite discord, pettiness, and anger. The lack of transparency is what makes it work. In school systems, the transparency requirement makes it nearly impossible to reward effort, contribution, and performance. Rewards are often reduced to objective data like test results, classes completed, and attendance, which rarely rewards all the best teachers. I'd love to be able to give a principal a bonus fund based on high performance (not just test scores) and ask them to develop a non-transparent plan to distribute it to teachers and other staff. I can just hear the outcry now, "That isn't fair!" But principals are closest to the action and know who is contributing, what they contribute, and how well they do it. I'm reminded of the aphorism, "All data is flawed. Some is useful." So is every compensation plan in a public setting. Might there be principals who reward friends? Possibly. But the answer isn't to make the whole process transparent. Giving supervisors discretion to reward their staff in ways that suit their culture and individual needs just makes sense.

From school boards I often hear, "Well, we would be better if we didn't have elected boards and could appoint better people." My answer: Nonsense. Education is a public enterprise, and locally elected officials are entrusted by the community to oversee it, connect with the public, and advocate for children's interests. The community chooses who will represent them. In business you need people who understand the organization's value and have complementary expertise. They aren't on the board to represent the public; they are lending their expertise to an enterprise they believe in and want to cultivate. As a leader it is critical to understand the context in which you are working and how to best engage your board members. Blocking and tackling (communication, framing challenges, reporting results) are the same, but specific plays are determined by your goals and optimal use of the talent and expertise on your board.

THE MAHONEY THREE

ONE: Schedule a ninety-minute board session to focus on communications between board members and the CEO. Consider having members take a social styles assessment administered by TRACOM. It outlines basic communication approaches and needs. Your report is personalized, and members will have a much better understanding and appreciation for how each member communicates based on their needs. The exercise will also create camaraderie.

TWO: Begin each board meeting with a special report delivered by different staff members on a topic of importance to the organization. The report may be used to highlight a success that the board isn't fully aware of, present an issue likely to be important in the future, or acknowledge a goal achieved. The point is to engage the board in discussion or celebration of work the staff is doing. People are down on what they aren't up on. This is an "up on" activity.

THREE: Host an annual "state of the organization" meeting for all stakeholders. Make it an opportunity to share successes, involve others, gather input, and help boards, staff, and stakeholders understand the work of the organization. Make it something people want to attend to learn, contribute, and feel engaged with important work.

Chapter 18

REALIZE CULTURE IS THE BYPRODUCT OF ALL YOU DO

Culture does not make people. People make culture.
CHIMAMANDA NGOZI ADICHIE

IN TEACHING IT DOESN'T TAKE LONG to understand how important a positive classroom culture is to student achievement and engagement. Attention to creating positive relationships, community building, meaningful conflict resolution, and understanding and appreciating differences pays off in the short and long term. These same culture-building efforts pay dividends in every aspect of life.

What Is Culture?

Culture is elusive. Culture has become a ubiquitous term to describe what you want or see. Whenever something good happens we ascribe it to cultural conditions. It turns out that the best culture is what is best for YOUR organization.

Business books abound with the sage advice that culture trumps strategy, meaning that the sum of who we are is more powerful than prescribed sets of action. Culture is palpable in organizations, on teams of all sorts, and certainly in school buildings. You can walk in and get a feeling almost immediately from an initial greeting, perhaps a sign, or just how things look. An organization's culture is reflected in everything they do. It's who they honor, what behaviors they accept or don't accept, who they include, what they celebrate, who they reward or don't, and all the rest. It's the cumulative set of actions that define the group. It's about the movie, not the scene. Culture is built piece by piece, action by action, over time.

If you want to understand the power of organizational culture, perhaps the best place to look is at schools. Above all, school should be a place where kids want to learn and teachers want to teach.

What I enjoyed most about my principalships was the chance to feed off the energy of the kids, watch teachers plan and execute engaging units, and create a sense of community. If I had a T-shirt to give to prospective principals it would say, "It's the culture, stupid."

Everything you do counts in some way. Whether you ask staff opinions or make all decisions yourself, stay in the office all day or walk the halls to be with students, visit classrooms only to evaluate or stop by to observe, communicate regularly or keep people in the dark, greet everyone in the morning when they arrive or simply look like you were weaned on a dill pickle—it all contributes to the culture you either intentionally build or let happen. Either way, that culture becomes the root system for the organization.

What is culture? Everything. Let's break that down. A consultant I admired would get at culture by asking people in an organization to fill in this blank: "Around here, we _____." The big rocks usually come quick with responses like, "work extraordinarily hard," "care about people," and "treat each other like family." Culture is indeed what you do, what you emphasize, what leaders model day-to-day, what you celebrate, and how you actually treat employees and clients or teachers and students. It is not what you say. It is what you do. My favorite high school principal used to look at kids and say, "You can't talk your way out of something you behaved yourself into." Behavior determines culture, and when you act outside those lines you get pulled back.

Culture becomes your brand, what you are known for. I often ask superintendents before I speak to their staff at convocations, "What is your district known for or most proud of?" Answers range from award-winning high school bands to football championships, high test scores, and new buildings. You get insight into their culture, because these things represent what they value and where they place their energies. I also ask them to tell me about past heroes and heroines who worked for the district and whose names most people would recognize. Then, I get stories.

"Marilyn was a chorus teacher at the high school for twenty-eight years and died of cancer several years ago while still teaching. Scores of students came back to school to sing at her memorial service and give testimony to her enthusiasm, care, and remarkable passion."

"Don was an icon after serving for decades as a math teacher, coach, and then high school principal. He was always principled yet flexible, strong yet humble. He expected much but gave much. The school staff, students, and community revered him for his contributions, wisdom, and authenticity."

These stories provide a sense of the culture beyond the talking points of accomplishment. What and whom people tell stories about reveals who they are as a people, what they value, and what they expect of others.

What Culture Is Best?

What culture is best? Whatever creates maximum impact for your school or business.

A great tool to understand the components of culture is the theory of Invitational Education designed and applied by professors Betty Siegel and William Purkey nearly five decades ago. It applies to schools and any workplace. They identify five *P*s—policies, processes, programs, people, and places—that summon and develop human potential. Everything either enriches or chips away at the existing culture. Each of the five *P*s either build or destroy the intellectual, social, physical, emotional, or moral potential of the people who are part of that culture.

For schools it means making them the most inviting places in town. A place you want to lead. A place parents want to send their children. A place of learning. A place of joy and fun. Today there is a renewed emphasis on the importance of developing grit and resilience in kids. And while children should learn and practice determination, perseverance, and grit, let's not forget joy and fun. School should not be an ordeal that kids must overcome.

For businesses it means creating a place where employees find meaningful work, feel involved, and are proud to be a part of the organization. As we discussed in Chapter 14, the best culture supports three elements that motivate people to higher levels of performance: purpose, autonomy, and mastery.

Charles Duhigg offers this nugget from his research about culture. He says CEOs who adopt a commitment model believe that getting the culture right is more important than designing the best product. This commitment model outperforms the star model (where the company hires elite talent and gives them autonomy), the engineering model (where the focus is on solving problems), and the bureaucratic model (where the focus is on process and hierarchy). By enlisting the loyalty of employees, businesses that follow the commitment model are faster to go public and have higher profitability ratios.

So, what is that best culture? I suggest you ask yourself and others questions like these: if our organization were running on all cylinders, how would we know? What are the lubricants we need to run this engine that way? What do we want our workplace to look like? Feel like? Begin to capture in your head the culture you believe is most likely to get the results you want. Then, turn that theory into practice with real people and real results. No more case studies. Just real stuff that takes constant appraisal, adjustment (sometimes on the fly), and steadfast principles.

Think of it as an aquarium where you expect fish to grow or a farm where you want crops to flourish. You need to pay attention to the water, soil, container, weather—all those things that assist in creating the culture you believe will be successful. What's important is to realize what culture is not. It is not a single tactic or silver bullet. It's not wishful thinking. It is intentional actions to align your behavior with a theory of real change and performance.

Perhaps one of the most famous current cultures is that of Southwest Airlines, a company started and led by whiskey-drinking, chain-smoking Herb Kelleher, who, along with businessman Rollin King, infamously mapped out a business plan connecting three Texas cities on a cocktail napkin. The part many don't know is that this business plan was strikingly similar to one developed by another company that failed in San Francisco. Execution does matter, and culture influences execution. As Kelleher famously said, "If you ain't got culture, you ain't got shit." Stories abound about the playfulness, thoughtfulness, and generosity of Southwest. Much of the early days are outlined in Kelleher's biography, *Nuts*. Southwest is a classic case of taking your work seriously but yourself not so much.

To this day, I still try to fly Southwest. Not everyone enjoys their sense of humor. Once, as the plane was roaring down the runway for takeoff, an employee began chanting on the loudspeaker, "I think I can, I think I can."

I thought it was hilarious; the lady next to me, not so much. Another time I about jumped out of my skin when I opened an overhead compartment and found an employee lying down in it. "Oh," she said, "thanks for waking me up!" Amid the laughter she hopped down and began helping others.

So, how is Southwest doing today? Before the pandemic it was America's largest airline, carrying 130 million passengers per year. Business researcher Jim Collins cited Southwest as the best place to grow money with a single investment from 1973–2003 ($1,000 to $1M), and the stock since that time has continued to grow. Their simple belief is that if you treat employees right, they will treat passengers right, and shareholders will gain value. It starts and ends with culture.

James Sinegal, successful CEO at Costco from 1983 to 2012, embraced a notion similar to Herb Kelleher's: "Customers will never love a company until employees love it first." How did Costco do during his tenure? Your investment would have grown by 1,200 percent! That happens when leaders communicate caring, create circles of safety, and help their employees grow.

Gallup facilitators who teach engagement often ask class participants to describe one of their best days at work. Ask kids the same question about their best school day, and I can promise you that themes will be similar for both. Answers will come quickly: "working on an interesting, challenging project, often with others," "sharing a struggle," "completing an important assignment and receiving some recognition for it." It's all part of the culture you create.

Never forget that a great culture is fragile and needs constant attention and reinforcement. In his book *Start With Why: How Great Leaders Inspire Everyone to Take Action*, Simon Sinek writes that leaders influence how the culture goes, which often predicts whether the company thrives or stalls. He illustrates his point in another book, *Leaders Eat Last: Why Some Teams Pull Together and Others Don't*, by examining the rise and fall of Goldman Sachs.

Goldman Sachs was a company with a sterling reputation from the 1970s through the early '90s. Built on high standards of trust, it was quite difficult to become a partner in the organization; partners were expected to put company over self. Then they went public in 1999. And while culture sometimes can disappear overnight with new leadership—as I like to say, it takes a carpenter to build a barn, but any jackass can knock it down—it most often occurs more slowly, until the entity becomes something very different over time. That was the case with Goldman Sachs. Sinek describes it as when "we veer away from doing the right thing in favor of doing the thing that's right for me." When we shift from values of strong character, we are often headed down a rocky road. When he announced his resignation from Goldman Sachs after twelve years, Greg Smith wrote this editorial:

> The culture was the secret sauce that made this place great and allowed us to earn our clients' trust for 143 years. It wasn't just about making money; this alone will not sustain a firm for long. It had something to do with pride and belief in the organization. I am sad to say that I look around today and see virtually no trace of the culture that made me love working for this firm for many years. I no longer have the pride, or the belief. Leadership used to be about ideas, setting an example, and doing the right thing. Today, if you make enough money for the firm (and are not currently an ax murderer) you will be promoted into a position of influence... When the history books are written about Goldman Sachs, they may reflect that the current chief executive officer...lost hold of the firm's culture.

Powerful. Is it possible that a disgruntled employee could express a view like that and not be representative of the whole company? Of course.

But look around. Are people leaving? Missing more work? Contributing to declining performance? There are lots of signs when negative culture moves from fringe to mainstream, and by the time the signs are clear it is most often too late. When people lie, manipulate, and misbehave, we blame culture. School strikes, like the one I participated in early in my teaching career, often are the result of a negative culture where people feel disrespected, alienated, and divided. Remember the Penn State University football team? Or Enron? That's how important culture is to any organization. In fact, it's so talked about that Merriam-Webster made *culture* its word of the year in 2014. It matters.

Creating a Great Culture

In his brilliant and compelling story of the 1936 University of Washington rowing team that captured the Olympic gold medal in Berlin, Dan Brown attributes their success at least in part to "swing." He writes, quoting legendary coach George Pocock, "Therein lies the secret of successful crews: Their swing, that fourth dimension of rowing which can only be appreciated by an oarsman who has rowed in a swinging crew, where the run is uncanny and the work of propelling the shell a delight." It's the thing in rowing that is hard to achieve and define. And so is building a culture.

It sure would be easier if I listed a magazine article entitled "Five Simple Ways to Improve Your Culture," or a handy guide entitled *Four Essentials of a Healthy Culture*. I'm sure I could find resources like this, but like many of the most complex issues in life, it is easier to describe culture successfully than to build one. It's complicated. But there are a few steps you can take to ensure a strong, healthy culture that works.

MEASURE

My first suggestion to improve your organization's culture is a measurement tool. After all, you can't improve what you don't measure. Gallup's Q12 measures employee engagement, a proven indicator of performance. Businesses all over the world use this simple tool, and it can be accessed digitally for minimal cost. The twelve questions measure areas including clear role expectations, employees' ability to do what they do best, and opportunities for learning and growth. It gives you a starting point to make improvements. We gave it to our employees each year at Battelle for Kids and it moved our performance dial forward financially, culturally, and emotionally.

IDENTIFY

Study best workplaces and you will find many similarities: great working conditions, fair pay, support, sense of mission, and encouragement. No surprises there. But doing it week after week is difficult. A culture of engagement, energy, risk taking, candor, and caring is created by recognizing the actions that support these values and helping them happen again and again. Studying employee motivation, the McKinsey consulting company found the top three non-financial motivators were praise from managers, the chance to lead projects, and opportunities for career growth. These are articulated in Gallup's Q12 survey, for example: "In the last seven days, I have received recognition or praise for doing good work."

Candidly, several years ago I participated in the strangest conversation on education that I have ever experienced. I was invited to a discussion with charter schools about class size, use of guidance counselors, etc. Nothing unusual there. I'd had that conversation many times about most effective practices, class size, and budget limitations. But this was the first and only time I ever heard this conversation carried out with a profit motive.

I can still recall the distinguishing question: "If we lower class size too much or add counselors, it will restrict our profits profoundly." *What?* I wanted to scream. I thought, *Where in this conversation do we talk about student benefits?* Apparently, we didn't. It was so foreign that the deciding factor for whether to add more teachers or counselors was profit. I don't want to characterize all charter schools this way, but this was my experience on one occasion that offered a perspective I had never considered in the education arena.

Frankly, a culture that is hell-bent on focus can be detrimental. In a company too focused on profit, conversations and actions can easily become solely about sales and revenue, thereby ignoring innovation, service, and other ideas that ultimately improve focus.

I well remember being asked to speak at an annual school boards dinner in an affluent Ohio county with multiple districts. Before I spoke, each superintendent introduced their board and gave an overview of the most recent year in their district. One superintendent clearly spelled out his priority, repeating several times, "If it isn't about instruction, it isn't about anything." Really? I was a county superintendent at the time in another part of the state, and while I could respect his focus, it said little about other issues kids bring to school that demand our support. Maybe this discord struck me because I so frequently saw poverty, broken homes, and kids in need of socioemotional support. I saw a need for a different kind of culture. Culture starts with the leader: what they say, what priorities they fund, where they spend their time, and ultimately what they want to be known for.

EXPECTATIONS

Setting expectations that staff agree to is a great starting point for maintaining a great culture. At Battelle for Kids, we enlisted a hundred staff members to help us develop a set of common expectations for each other. I'd like to say that everyone on the staff immediately complied with these.

Some didn't, and I failed to enforce the expectations for some people. Not the easy, obvious things, of course, but it occurs bit by bit. It's like having and keeping a clean room. It's easy to leave one piece of clothing on a chair, and the room still looks good. Dust on the nightstand. Piece by piece clutter accumulates, when it would have been easier to address it early. Good teachers have clear expectations and enforce them regularly, and so do superior leaders. But they do it by empowering people, not simply directing them.

INVEST

Did you ever just walk into a place and feel the energy? It may have started in an entryway with colored walls, interesting artwork, or a warm greeting by a friendly face as soon as you entered. One of the best investments we ever made at Battelle for Kids was in late 2004, in preparation for our move to a new location previously occupied by a technology company. The eight thousand square feet had dozens of workstations that looked like study carrels, a handful of conference rooms, and several individual offices. At the time there were twelve of us, so we had plenty of space, but we also wanted to carve out a large conference room for trainings, think about future growth of staff, and create proximity among folks who worked together on various projects.

Our investment? A design engineer. She spent time with us to understand how we worked as a team, our likes and dislikes, our vision for the future, and how we wanted our new place to feel. She was charged with redefining our space but really got to know us before creating her design, which we ultimately followed to a tee. She got all the functional parts right, but most importantly she captured the energy. Over the years, visitors would comment on the brightly colored walls and energetic feel of the place. It motivated all of us, too. It began with a workplace specifically designed to meet our needs. Revolutionary? Hardly. Common practice?

Maybe. But it matters. Invest in strategies that keep teams moving and improving together.

PRACTICE

Bridgewater Associates handles billions of dollars in investments and lives the philosophy outlined by its founder. The principles have been downloaded two million times:

> Bridgewater's competitive edge is our pioneering workplace culture that relies on truthful and transparent communication to ensure the best ideas win out. We believe meaningful work and meaningful relationships emerge when you assemble high-performing teams and push them to engage in rigorous and thoughtful inquiry.
>
> We champion diversity because it is essential to our ability to think differently. We cultivate inclusion because we believe people do their best work when they can be their genuine selves. By continually examining abilities and performance, we provide all our employees with the development they need to fulfill their potentials as professionals and people.

One example of living the Bridgewater philosophy is avoiding groupthink and inviting counter opinions. It's like another of my favorite sayings: If two people agree on everything, one is useless. If they disagree on everything, they are both useless. It's in the meaningful and honest exchange of ideas that we grow.

In a great culture, an organization takes its mission statement seriously and practices what it preaches every day. When you remind people in word and deed that your work is tied to a higher purpose, you make it part of the culture. But you have to do it repeatedly, consistently, and authentically. That's what great teachers and leaders do. You want employees to feel like their work matters—that it contributes to something higher than themselves, just as great teachers connect work to learning. In both cases, long after they have forgotten the assignment, people remember the love of contributing, serving, and learning. This is only achieved with intentionality.

What kind of culture do you want? Build it through actions and expectations. I have found this maxim to be quite true: you get what you give. If you want people to have enthusiasm, you need to be enthusiastic. If you want people to work hard, you need to work hard. You can't just say it. You must also do it. Great leaders don't write one-time memos any more than great teachers give one-time lectures. Show and do repeatedly. Rinse and repeat!

ENERGY

Energy is a combination of enthusiasm, vitality, and a feeling of moving forward. One of my longstanding strengths from the Clifton StrengthsFinder is "activator." Activators are the people who often say, "When can we start?" They want to do something, not wait for the complete analysis or removal of risk. This is not to suggest that energy is only created by activators; leaders can use their individual strengths to move people. Others may get people to think about the future or generate new ideas. My experience is that whatever emotion you give, others get. My enthusiasm often generated enthusiasm from others, and we had a physical workplace that subtly encouraged this all day. Energy is about taking positive action, learning as you go, and changing on the fly.

Microsoft used to give a creativity test to managers and MBA students. They gave them uncooked spaghetti, string, and tape, and asked them to build the tallest structure they could and place a marshmallow at the top.

Who did it best: managers or MBA students? Neither. The best performers were kindergartners who just jumped right in, unafraid of failure, and began doing, learning, failing, and correcting right away. That is positive energy. You can't wait to get started. You are motivated to use your strengths to perform important tasks. It's really hard to separate the leader from the organization; an energized leader creates more energy, more action, and yes, more mistakes. But you learn from them and move on.

I once hired a consultant who had successfully led a technology company through phenomenal growth. I asked him to spend a couple months with us at Battelle for Kids, review our financials, go to any meeting he wanted, interview anyone he wanted, and come back to me and our senior team with a list of recommendations for how we could get better. After all, I wasn't a business guy, and this was a business. I was afraid that I would miss something and do a tremendous disservice to our staff.

Dan was terrific and came back with a series of recommendations that made sense. We shared them with our board and staff and (remember my "activator" strength) did implement them. But it was this conversation with him that I remember most. He asked, "How do people get their jobs here?"

"Many are referred by folks who work here. We advertise and use our networks to actively recruit people we think might be most likely to help us," I answered.

After a few more queries, he offered this summary. "You may not all be of the same church here, but you are of the same religion. And it's awfully hard to get into this church unless you are."

"What do you mean?" I said.

"I mean you don't ultimately get hired here if you don't believe in the mission, aren't energized to action, and can't work proactively to get things done."

"What's wrong with that?"

"I didn't say it was a problem, only a clear observation after seeing and talking to people for several months. It could be a blind spot if you are all alike and not open to new ideas and approaches, but I didn't detect that."

The people who worked there shared a positive energy. It was a reminder that the staff reflects the characteristics of the leader, and the leader shapes the culture. I was encouraged by his comments. As a startup, we needed people who took risks, felt empowered to act, and acted. But the characteristics that got us to that point were not the same ones required to get where we needed to be. As we grew, scaled, and learned, we indeed needed more structure, clearer lines of authority, and protocols—in other words, more order to our chaotic world. Organizations need different types of leadership based on where they are in their evolution, and leaders should tap into different sides of themselves to support that process.

People Make Up the Culture

You might think having the right group of people is enough to create and maintain a great culture in your organization. But we've all experienced the deadening of spirit in a negative culture and the energizing of spirit in a great culture. People avoid participating when they feel threatened and unappreciated. Those same people thrive in cultures where they feel safe and part of something bigger than themselves. They don't want to let other colleagues down.

Laura Carstensen, a Stanford researcher, studied the emotional experiences of people at different ages, from eight to ninety-three. One thing was clear: perspective matters, not age. How you see things. And I'd argue that how you see things is how you do things. The *Wall Street Journal* reported that some of our country's most successful innovators (Jeff Bezos of Amazon, Larry Page and Sergey Brin of Google, and Jimmy Wales of Wikipedia) all attended Montessori schools that emphasize collaboration, self-direction, questioning, motivation—a culture of innovation, not test taking. A culture can inhibit or celebrate the perspective that people bring to it.

The need to have the right people for the job is pretty obvious. How to *find* the right people is a lot less obvious. I found them most often by consulting our own staff, those who best knew the climate, expectations, and work, and they suggested people they felt were of the same mindset and abilities. But people aren't fungible commodities. Hiring my own staff at Battelle for Kids was both a luxury and a great responsibility. Each new hire with their unique personality could dramatically impact the culture, and we were shaping the culture as we went.

Finding the right people isn't enough. I think Gallup had it right when they wrote, "Hire for talent, develop for fit, and motivate by strength." I've watched the entire human capital dimension play out—finding, recruiting, placing, developing, nurturing, supporting, compensating, and evaluating. Too often people suggest that hiring the right people and getting out of their way is sufficient. What's the old phrase—even eagles need a push? As CEO, I was constantly conscious of supporting people through feedback and "management by walking around." I never worried about early expectations because I gave the same short talk just prior to a job offer. I made sure that I had the final conversation with each person hired, and I always reserved the right to simply not make an offer. I also did not impose new people on teams without their input.

My short conversation before employment went like this: "There are three things I insist upon if you work here. The first is that you work hard. People will work eight hours a day for a paycheck, ten hours a day for a good boss, and twenty-four hours a day for a good cause. We have a good cause here, and while I don't ask people to work crazy hours, there will be those times that helping a client, getting ready for a conference, or preparing a grant will require extra time and effort, and you need to do that. If you ever say, 'That's not in my job description,' you are probably in the wrong place.

"The second expectation is that you play well with others. That doesn't mean to capitulate or never disagree. In fact, just the opposite. I expect honest disagreement and full disclosure about what you think. But it needs to be done openly, honestly, and authentically. Duplicity, backstabbing, and 'isn't that nice' have no place here. We are in this together. If the front end of the boat is leaking, it's not just the front end that will be harmed."

My third expectation, always at the end, began with this question. "Do you want this job?" I wanted to hear from them that yes, it was what they wanted, and why. If their response was satisfactory, I extended a hand and offered the job officially. We had that sweet moment of joy. Do you remember job offers you took because you wanted that job? Were you excited? Couldn't wait to start? I don't subscribe to the theory that staff have to lose that excitement. They don't. It matures, of course, from that puppy peeing, tail wagging moment to smiling and appreciating what you do, who you do it with, and why you do it. And the leader's role is to have a vested interest in the success of that employee from the moment you make that offer. The financial and emotional costs are too high if you pay no attention to that person.

Here are two real reactions I received after that speech. In one case, I asked a young graphic designer when she could start. She smiled and said sincerely, "I can be ready in thirty minutes!" And she remains enthusiastic and terrific in her work to this day. In the other case, when I asked if the interviewee wanted this job, I got a rather halfhearted acceptance. I queried further, and she clarified, "I thought this job might be a little better than my current one." I didn't offer her the job. I went back to the team leader who had recommended her and asked, "Is this the best person we could find for this position?" He sheepishly admitted that she was a compromise candidate that he wasn't excited about either. So we started the process over to find someone with the skills, talents, and motivation to be there. People don't have to jump up and down when you ask, "Do you want this job?" But they should have sufficient and authentic reasons why they want to be there.

Can an organization be too large to pay attention to individuals? Never. Sure, if you are CEO of United Way or a large bank in a major city, you can't possibly know, interview, and make job offers to everyone. But every organization has layers of leaders, and you can insist that leaders at each level know their people. What you pay attention to, how you treat people, and how you listen to employees will speak volumes about you and will spread throughout your organization. For the life of me, I can't figure out how anyone thinks that the treatment of your workforce doesn't impact your performance. A steady diet of fear, anxiety, and intimidation rarely offers long-term organizational success.

When hiring, consider not only individual qualifications but also how new employees will work as part of a team. Do they have the necessary work ethic, enthusiasm, and ability to play well with others?

**Customers will never love a company
until the employees love it first.**
SIMON SINEK

THE MAHONEY THREE

ONE: Do an organizational culture check. Give each person a stoplight handout. Next to the red light, list two things the organization should stop doing. For green, list two practices that are working well. For yellow, list two things the organization should reexamine to determine whether they still have value. Be prepared to share results and act where you can. (Note, this activity is expanded on in the following chapter.)

TWO: Dr. William Purkey, cofounder of Invitational Education, has written extensively about using blue and orange as organizational metaphors. Anything that is beneficial and adds value is blue; detrimental practices are orange. Brainstorm blue and orange practices, processes, and behaviors in small groups. Discuss these practices, particularly the ones that add value.

THREE: Do a 3-2-1 activity to assess a current culture change. After a new practice has been in place for a month or so, ask: what are three things that are working with this practice? What are two questions you have about it? What is one remaining challenge? Collect the responses and, if needed, ask different questions. The 3-2-1 activity is about garnering feedback to refine and improve any process.

Chapter 19

WORK CONSTRUCTIVELY IN TEAMS

When you want to go fast, go alone.
When you want to go far, go together.
AFRICAN PROVERB

EFFECTIVE TEACHERS learn how to motivate students to work in teams. There are so many benefits. Not only does a productive team foster creativity, engagement, and trust, it can teach conflict resolution and promote healthy risk taking. Productive teamwork is challenging when there is conflict or when some members don't pull their weight. Those team-building skills learned in the classroom apply every time people work together.

People make up a culture and, in many organizations, people work in teams. Then teams of people make up the culture. Some teams are competitive and some work toward a common goal. As students, we team up on projects, in sports, or for common interests. Teachers may be part of grade-level or subject-area teams. Most people have had both good and bad experiences with teams.

Try this sometime with a group: ask them to describe the best team they ever played with. Some will choose athletic teams, others a project-based work team. Notice how the emotional quality of their description is impacted by the team leader. I like how rowing coach George Pocock describes rowing as "the losing of self entirely to the cooperative effort of the crew as a whole." This is what it feels like when a team really gels. If you do this exercise with a group, you'll be hard pressed to find successful teams that were not influenced greatly by their leader—keeping in mind that the leader may not be the one formally in charge. Good leaders know exactly when to let go so that can happen.

Again, it's that paradox. What you like is what you don't like. I like working with, for, and on behalf of other people. There is a certain energy created by people working together on mutual projects. But I don't like the complexity that comes with it—petty disputes, lack of follow-through, soloists, and duplicity committed by the same people. To be clear, I've done my share of creating excitement, but in overexuberance or moments of impatience, treating people in ways that weren't exactly encouraging or motivating. But our imperfection is part of our humanity.

Adam Grant has researched one of the great entertainment teams, the founding cast of *Saturday Night Live* chosen by longtime director and producer Lorne Michaels. Dan Aykroyd. John Belushi. Gilda Radner. Michaels invited and even encouraged dissent. The environment had tension and strengths. He created a sort of psychological safety net for people to argue with one another yet be there for one another—all at the same time. This is an essential component of successful teams.

Decide which team you want to be on. Team A has eight women and two men—all smart and successful. They are polite, articulate, and courteous. They take turns speaking and don't interrupt when an expert in the group speaks on a particular subject. The meeting is efficient, on task, and on time. Team B is evenly divided between men and women including successful executives and middle managers without many accomplishments to date.

Their members are curt at times, interrupt at others, and ramble on occasion. When someone goes off topic, the others easily follow. The meeting doesn't really end as much as trail off as people sit around gossiping.

Which team do you want to join? Let's start with empathy. Team B achieved empathy 58 percent of the time, while A weighed in at 49 percent. Teams succeed not because of the innate qualities of individual members, but because of how they treat one another. Team B is clearly messier, but when the group unites, the sum is greater than its parts. Team A has smart people but little evidence that they are collectively more intelligent. Grant says that good teams share two important qualities: members speak roughly in the same proportion, and they test high in social sensitivity. They intuit how members feel based on tone of voice, expression, etc. Pick Team B. They have created the essential quality of the founding cast of SNL—psychological safety. I always ask my teams: what can we do better together than we could do individually? The juice has to be worth the squeeze!

Google has also weighed in on team selection and effectiveness. Their 2015 research suggested that how teams work is more important than who is on them. You don't need superstars, but effective teams will believe their work is important and personally meaningful, have clear goals and defined roles, know they can depend upon one another, and have psychological safety.

Keys to Working Successfully on Teams

DON'T ASSUME MOTIVATION

The single best advice I ever got was simple: don't assume the motivations of others. It gets us into trouble when we ascribe the behavior of others to nefarious motives and, by extension, their darkest sides. Our heads begin to play tapes with sentences like, "They don't want this to work because it wasn't their idea"; "He isn't contributing much because he's mad that he isn't in charge"; or "She just can't live with someone else besting her." We are fighting a losing battle when we go down this road.

Self-talk can work for or against us. I have a colleague who embodies this advice. She sincerely, consistently, and honestly doesn't judge people. She always sees the good in others. And guess what? She finds it, and it's why people want to work with her on projects. Suspending judgment of others is an easy concept to understand, but practicing it will save you a lot of grief, time, and toxic self-talk!

GIVE CREDIT TO OTHERS

Here's a second piece of sage advice in working with teams: give credit to others, and do it sincerely, easily, and often. The power of affirmation has long been proven. People will work for a compliment, a notice of effort, or similar acknowledgment. Legendary University of Alabama football coach Bear Bryant once noted, "If things go bad, I did it. If things go okay, we did it. If things go great, they did it." I can easily list the technical aspects of teams working together—developing goals, assigning responsibilities, creating focus, and all the rest. But the glue that holds them together, especially in adversity, the lubricant that keeps them moving, and the joy that comes from working in teams is found in our most human of emotions: simple appreciation.

But humans don't all respond to the same kind of appreciation. How do you know, then, whether someone wants a note of quiet acknowledgment or a public statement of their good work? Ask them. "If you do something really well, how would you like to be acknowledged?" I have done that, insisting on a reply that I won't share with others but promise to practice with them. Some say, "Pay me more," others like public acknowledgment with the board, and still others want you to tell them directly and give them more of that kind of work. Let me re-emphasize what we covered previously: When it comes to motivation, one size doesn't fit all. In fact, some folks hate public acknowledgment and become dissatisfied when you do it. Here we have a variation of the golden rule: don't treat people the way you want to be treated. Treat them the way *they* want to be treated.

Invent ways to honor and thank teams, groups, and individuals. Truly, what gets rewarded gets done. I always started each board meeting with a positive report of what some team was doing on behalf of children. It might be an established group like the district guidance department or an invented group, like the first-grade teachers at several elementary schools reporting on a day in the life of a first grader. Every board meeting would start with this report no matter how many were present. The first twenty minutes we heard from some person or team doing important work on behalf of children. Board members asked questions, learned from the report, and acknowledged their work with portfolios or some other small gift presented at the end. It was a chance to not only celebrate the work of a team but to set the tone for the entire meeting. Even visitors who were there to challenge the board on some issue were softened, I'm sure, by the story and tone of the positive presentation, discussion, and thank you. This practice was consistent and became part of the culture—we did it every month at the regular meeting.

COMMUNICATE

As a principal I got a much larger view of the world with so many things going on at the same time. I worried that my staff would not know what was going on, so I began my lifelong practice of writing weekly memos. Each Monday morning, I would write a note about things happening that week, congratulations and thank yous, ideas to think about, and other tidbits. I carried this habit through every job I had after that principalship. People like being in the know and having ideas to talk about, and it focuses energy for the week. My mantra has always been, "People are down on what they aren't up on." This is your chance to inform, initiate, and inspire. Every week.

This tool needs to be in everyone's toolbox. After all, school isn't just a place. What matters most is what is *taking place*.

In fact, as I think about that principalship, I realize that I would approach that job today the same as I did then. Know the people who work there. Listen to them. Build trust by following through and keeping confidences. Meet parents. Understand the context. Decide what to expect. Communicate. Manage. Lead. Remember that one simple approach to communication is to use a stoplight framework. Ask each staff member what is good and shouldn't be changed (green), what is not so good and should be stopped (red), and what they aren't sure about (yellow). I promise you that after these short individual conferences you will know people better, have a strong sense of the context, and be clear on your next steps. The time it takes will pay off in the long run. Sometimes to go fast, you need to go slow. But slow is not interminable!

CULTIVATE STRENGTHS

Teams thrive when their individual members are able to use and cultivate their strengths. Gallup's StrengthsFinder tool has been used by over twenty million people across the globe. I've used it with students many times, and they, like me, have their own personal *aha* moments after getting their results. It describes who you are. Now, after all these years, I can see why I liked creating ideas, encouraging others to buy into them, and then initiating activity. I was doing what I liked! I was using my strengths. Maybe this accounts for why Denmark is one of the happiest places on the planet. People there are committed to purpose. Students may take up to seven years to finish college. In that way they are more likely to find their passion—their calling, if you will. Are workers who are actively engaged, their passions fueled and strengths used, likelier to be happier, more productive, and to spread positivity? Duh!

COLLABORATE

Fifteen years ago I had a heart attack; six months later I had open heart surgery. At the time I was a very healthy fifty-two-year-old. I worked out several times a week, ran half marathons, didn't smoke, and was an average weight for my height. Still, after a catheterization and report of arterial blockages, I accepted the recommendation to have surgery. I met with the surgeon the next day. Imagine what you would ask your surgeon in this case. Of course, "Have you done this procedure many times?" I didn't want someone opening my chest and saying, "Hey, is this how it's supposed to look?" You get the idea. This routine question led to a revelation.

Research conducted by Hauptman and Pisanto set out to answer my question. They wanted to know specifically if surgeons got better with practice. They tracked forty thousand bypass procedures performed by two hundred cardiac surgeons at forty-three hospitals. Overall, they didn't get better with practice. Take that in as I did. What? They did get better at specific hospitals where they practiced with the same team. Risk there dropped to 1 percent from 3 percent at other hospitals. But they didn't carry performance with them. A similar study was done in the financial sector with investors. Stars in that field didn't carry performance with them either unless they stayed with the same team. Collaboration—both the actions you take and the understanding you gain from knowing your team's strengths and weaknesses—is essential to growth.

LAUGH

I'll say it again: if you can't laugh at yourself, you leave the job to everyone else! School and any workplace should be a place for laughter, genuine warmth, and community. Leaders largely determine whether there is a culture of joy or dread. Let's face it. You couldn't make up the things that routinely occur in schools. And laughter should be *with* folks, never at them. During my first game as a junior high basketball coach, in the middle of the second quarter I told a kid to go into the game for another player. He just jumped off the bench and went straight into the game without checking in at the scorer's table. The referee stopped the game. I realized he had never played in an organized game before and didn't know that this is what you had to do. That same game I had another seventh grader start to get dressed at half time. I asked him what he was doing, and he simply replied, "Isn't it over?" This of course was all my fault and I could laugh easily with kids as I took the blame. You can't make this stuff up.

Make Team Meetings Count

Too often leaders overlook perhaps their most important constituency: their own staff. Worse yet, staff meetings can become an afterthought when they are held irregularly, little thought is given to meeting outcomes, and they are seen as an obligation rather than an opportunity. I used to jokingly say at meetings, "Nothing is impossible for those who don't have to do the work." I'm a true believer in carefully recruiting and selecting staff but developing them along the way, and how you engage them at staff meetings is particularly important. Ask yourself, "What do I want from staff meetings?" This is the opportunity for the CEO and other senior leadership to connect personally to the people who make things happen on your behalf. It's your chance as a leader to teach successfully. And the size of your staff doesn't matter. People want to be "in the know," to be part of something bigger than themselves, and to contribute in meaningful ways. Staff meetings can reinforce all those things.

I was fortunate to work with assistants over the years who felt the same way and planned engaging meetings for staff to be in the know, share ideas, ask questions, feel appreciated, and leave energized by prospects ahead of them. I've also witnessed obligatory meetings where leaders simply applied what some call the "mushroom theory" of leadership—keep people in the dark and feed them crap. In other meetings, staff are told things, never engaged, and everyone including the leaders feel obligated to go and listen, as opposed to being excited to attend and motivated when they leave. Planning for the staff meeting is critical if you want to keep your workers engaged. Ask yourself first, "When this meeting is over, what do I want people to know that they may not know at all, or need to know more about?" Second, "How do I want them to feel after this meeting?" And third, "What do I want them to do?"

Much of what you do at a staff meeting is contextual. If you are considering a change in strategic direction or adding a new service, why wouldn't you get input from folks who regularly do the work? The more I give staff members chances to weigh in on things they know about, the more I solidify their efforts to make our work successful. Whatever you are hearing, trust me—they are likely hearing it too. Let them help you help the organization. This is where the plural pronouns—*we, us*, and *our*—are brought to fruition. I can promise you that when you successfully engage staff they will be more energized and productive going forward. Make staff meetings count—what do you want employees to *know, feel*, and *do*?

A staff member once teased me that if my administration were an American presidency, it would be James Monroe's, whose terms were known as "the era of good feeling." So be it, as long as one understands that creating a culture that emphasizes teamwork, supports autonomy, and celebrates success is also totally consistent with tackling difficult challenges, solving intractable problems, and producing results. In fact, I would argue that such a culture facilitates success with the latter.

Resolving Inevitable Conflicts

You can't have people working together without inevitable conflicts, but you can escalate or de-escalate those conflicts with your actions. There is an old Latin phrase: "See everything. Overlook a lot. Improve a little." Pretty good advice. But again, the culture will be heavily influenced by where you focus attention.

I learned a lot about conflicts that result in school strikes. They rarely benefit anyone and leave scars that often take a generation to diminish but never remove. Even if it's just a day. When superintendents are faced with a strike, the business community says, "Hang in there. Don't give in to unrealistic demands." But if the strike actually occurs, these same people quickly say, "You have to solve this. It's killing the community." My advice is to solve it before it happens—not by giving in to demands that you can't honor, or by negotiating to give less than you could. Alienating your entire workforce is not a good strategy for anything. That's why skills, experience, and positive approaches work. Fortunately, school strikes are extraordinarily rare today. I would urge teachers and administration to keep at negotiations until they are settled rather than live with the prolonged disruption and hard feelings that inevitably accompany a strike. Then the toothpaste is out of the tube and you can't put it back.

People don't see the same thing the same way, even when it comes to events where both sides completely agree on what happened. Early on, I thought my job was to resolve conflict. Because I believed that and acted on it, there was no shortage of problems and emotions to calm on any given day. A kid misbehaved on the bus. This teacher disagrees with the grading approach of other teachers or the location of the next field trip. Along with simple problems like these are more serious ones like calling children's services because a child has reported troubling things happening to them at home, or a colossal custody battle between parents that has now spilled over into school. I was policeman, referee, and ombudsman rolled into one and spent considerable time unwinding scenarios, imperfectly rendering judgment, and generally becoming the lightning rod for disputes. As I saw it, my job was to troubleshoot and solve disputes quickly, or even better to suppress conflict altogether. It doesn't work. The only one who gets an ulcer is you. When conflict couldn't be suppressed, I eventually owned it, not the folks who were having the dispute. The good news is that the groups fighting often became united against the common enemy—me!

Here is what I came to learn about conflict. It is a natural consequence of people interacting together. I later came to promote it, as disagreements are best understood in the open without personalities attached to them. I started having the "parking lot conversations" at staff meetings. No more going to the parking lot or to meetings after the meeting to say what you should have said earlier. The leader's role here is key: you have to make it safe to disagree publicly among staff. Only through this kind of dialogue can people grow, understand other perspectives, and solve problems.

I learned this wasn't my school or my business. This was our organization, and real ownership comes from solving problems collectively, not calling on the leader to take sides. Is there a time for the leader to take a stand? Absolutely: when there is a value at stake, like our beliefs about how we grade, reward, or punish students. But the robust discussion beforehand is critical to clarify where people stand. I also learned that time and urgency go together. Not all problems are equal. Dealing with a recalcitrant student is not the same as handling a bomb threat. In Stephen Covey's parlance, part of the leader's role is to place urgency and importance in perspective. You can waste way too much time on unimportant, non-urgent items. And how you spend your time ultimately defines you as a leader.

Remember to look at a problem from somebody else's perspective. Seek to understand. For example, I had a lovely older teacher stop by my office to say her class pencil sharpener wasn't working properly. Pretty simple, right? And completely mishandled by me. Her problem came in the midst of a bus driver dragging two kids to my office and screaming at them for fighting, a parent yelling at me because he thought a teacher had mistreated his child, and someone from the central office asking why I had not turned in a bureaucratic form they needed for who-knows-what. You get the picture. There was high-octane emotion exploding everywhere, and befitting my style and Irish temper, I escalated the temperature. This wonderful teacher whom I admired greatly came to me with a simple, polite request to fix or replace her pencil sharpener. And what did I do? Did I say, "I'm sorry. I will ask the custodian to see what he can do about it. I know what an annoyance that can be when you have children who need to sharpen pencils. Thanks for letting me know." Nope. Instead I offered this miserable reaction. "Do I *look* like the guy in charge of pencil sharpeners? Is this what you think I should be doing? Go find a custodian or someone who can help you!" In other words, *I'm having a bad morning and you should get the hell out of here.* She did. And when things calmed down, I apologized to her and took care of it.

But no matter how many times I apologized, it never made up for my poor treatment of her in a single angry moment. I still remember it. While my response may be understandable in context, it was way out of proportion. And I can promise you this: even lovely people don't forget hostile acts like this, and they take a long time to forgive you. It's like pulling a nail out of a fine piece of wood. It can be removed, but it never looks the same.

As a leader, you will have those times when it is all coming at you. Take a deep breath. Phone a friend. Think. Sometimes it's not only okay but preferable to let a little grass grow before responding. That is why control of your emotions, understanding of the situation, and problem-solving skills matter. What happens in our personal lives impacts how we show up in our professional lives. Be a leader who supports others, creates a culture of comfort, and extends time to heal when people need it. Create the culture you want for yourself.

Probably the quickest way to de-escalate conflict is to agree with someone or find humor in a situation. Once I had an argument with a strong-willed veteran teacher who was more than irritated with my resolution. I placed half a Snickers bar in her mailbox with a note. I knew when she would most likely come to her mailbox, so I waited in the office to see her reaction. She took the torn candy bar and read the attached note: "Please eat this as perhaps it will sweeten you up. Jim. Turn over." You could see her visceral reaction, but fortunately she turned it over. On the other side I had written, "I ate the other half." I saw her laugh and came out of the office where I had been watching. We laughed together. Once again, if it is done authentically and appropriately, laughter can be the shortest distance between two people.

Surprise and agreement can also defuse a volatile situation. I had a superintendent friend relate how he handled an escalating situation with a parent. The father of a sixth grader was upset by the grading practices and treatment of his son by a middle school teacher. He insisted on speaking to the superintendent and unloaded his displeasure over the telephone, becoming progressively angrier as he spoke. "How can you and the principal accept this teacher's behavior? Why don't you do something?"

The superintendent responded calmly, "I understand what you are saying, and I would feel the same way if it were my child saying he was treated like that. I'll find out and handle it."

It wasn't enough. The man kept his diatribe going. "You know, the same thing happened two years ago to my brother's son when he was in the sixth grade. Nobody did *anything*," he said, his voice rising. Finally, in exasperation the parent threatened, "I think I am just going to get my brother and we are going to come to your office and kick your ass!"

Now the superintendent, who didn't know the parent, asked back: "Have you ever met me?"

There was a short silence as the parent considered what the superintendent might look like (quite likely, how big he was). "No," he said.

The superintendent added calmly, "You don't need your brother." It took the guy a few seconds to process and then he began to laugh. Of course, humor doesn't always work to defuse conflict, but it can be an effective tool if you know when and how to use it.

How you handle conflict, the community you build, the celebrations you hold are all part of the culture you create. A staff that can laugh, argue, and cry together can do anything. For a principal, there is nothing more challenging, fear producing, engaging, or frustrating than this role, and sometimes all these emotions can be felt in a single morning. But never doubt that you matter. Just think about the best place you ever worked or the best team you played on. I'm willing to bet that both the leader and culture mattered a great deal. And while there is no perfect mix of people, there are practices that can make your organization a place where people want to be and perform well while they're there.

So, how do you avoid waiting for the building to burn? Use surveys like the Gallup Q12. Provide rich opportunities for two-way communication. Promote transparency. Work on the work. Address issues. Make improvement part of the culture. Be able to answer the prompt, "Around here we know what is happening because _____." People and their behaviors are the culture. People are not fungible. Conflict is inevitable. Creating a safe space to disagree and see each others' perspectives is a critical element of healthy workplace culture. We are all humans first.

Explore culture with staff, parents, and kids by asking, "What kind of place do you want this to be? What would a great school look like? How would you know it was great?" I would argue that education or business reform starts and ends with this question: "What is our purpose here?" These questions help you to envision a great culture. Benjamin Mays noted, "The tragedy of life is not a failure to reach your goal. It is having no goal to reach."

Leadership ultimately is not about what you believe, but what you do—the actions you take to build strong teams, motivate others, develop relationships, and by extension, build culture.

Lastly, I would challenge every educator or employer with this fundamental question: *Would you want your child to attend school or work here?* The answer must be yes. If it isn't, make it a place where the answer can be yes. You have both the power and responsibility to make it a great place for children to grow, learn, and yes, become.

Whatever the best parent wants for his child, the community should want for all its children.
JOHN DEWEY

THE MAHONEY THREE

ONE: A common problem of teams, intentional or not, is siloing—not knowing what the others in your group are doing. Assign a color to each member of your senior team and give them a glass full of crayons in their color. In a school district central office, you may give the special education director blue crayons, the early childhood director green, etc. Ask them to place their glass on their desk, easily visible to visitors. When leaders from different departments have a substantive conversation, they trade crayons. It's a visual indicator of whether you are talking with others. Are you accumulating crayons of different colors in your glass, or not? You can periodically inspect the glasses for movement.

TWO: Send a weekly team memo to your staff. People are down on what they aren't up on! Keep it short but use it to introduce ideas on the horizon, thank yous and congratulations, reminders, etc. It creates a bond among team members. As a variation, assign the weekly memo to other team members, encouraging them to acknowledge others and stay on top of things by being responsible for it that week.

THREE: Ask members of your team to think about the best team they were ever on—athletic, organizational, social, etc. Why did they pick that team? Identify common characteristics from everyone's experience. Make up a survey asking people to rate their current team's performance based on the characteristics of successful teams they've identified. For those rated high, ask the team why. For those rated low, ask how they might improve.

Chapter 20
IT'S ALL ABOUT SALES

To sell well is to convince someone else to part
with resources—not to deprive that person,
but to leave him better off in the end.
DANIEL PINK

AS A TEACHER, I learned how to sell. I sold students on becoming engaged in learning about social studies. I sold parents on my commitment to their children. I sold other teachers and my principal on my reliability. I learned to develop the qualities of extraordinary salespeople, including product knowledge, passion, organization, self-motivation, and the ability to develop strong relationships. And I've applied these qualities to my leadership roles as well.

Daniel Pink's book *To Sell Is Human* argues that we are nearly all in sales in one way or another. While I was a superintendent, I ran into an old sales buddy of mine at an honorary luncheon for one of our elementary schools. I recognized his name in the program, and I decided to see if it was the same guy I remembered from the '60s. We had worked together selling magazines door-to-door in high school (this was long before local laws prohibiting door-to-door sales). I still remember the deal: customers got five magazine subscriptions for thirty-five cents a week with a five-year agreement. I cringe now when I think about going door-to-door, but at the time I really enjoyed selling. That second summer I won a sales contest and received an all-expense-paid trip to the 1967 World's Fair in Montreal, Canada.

When the lunch concluded, I went over and immediately recognized him, as he did me. I told him I was now a superintendent.

"You are a school superintendent?" he asked incredulously. "I always thought you would be in sales!"

"I am!" I said.

Pink was right. We are all in sales. I had used my door-to-door skills as a teacher to sell social studies to seventh and eighth graders, as a principal to sell my ideas to staff, and as a superintendent to sell levies and our brand of education to the community. Soon I'd be using those same skills to develop a successful business in social entrepreneurism.

A sale may or may not involve money, and people acquire goods or services based on emotional needs or wants. When a seller connects with people and their emotional reasons for wanting things, they have tremendous power to give people what they want and make them feel great about their purchase. They key is convincing the buyer to take the plunge, whether you're selling a magazine, getting students to do their homework, convincing teachers to use a new curriculum, or persuading a community to raise taxes to support a new school building.

Value Proposition

Sales involves creating goods and services that people want to acquire, and that involves figuring out what makes something valuable to a potential buyer. Successful enterprises know their value proposition, a statement that describes the benefits of their product. For example, attending your school:

what makes your school a better choice than the alternatives? How does your school help families solve problems or fulfill their desires? This is what we do and why we do it.

Organizations use their value proposition to communicate with their workforce and reinforce their brand with customers. If I said to you, "Who makes the very best cars in the world? Or the best phones?" Names of companies immediately pop into your head because of personal experience, brand recognition, or longstanding evidence. But it starts with purpose. Why do you exist? What are you delivering that offers customers something of distinct value? Your discussion and decisions around your value proposition will create clarity, and clarity keeps the road to success smoother, wider, and free of obstacles.

Simon Sinek was spot-on with the title of his bestselling book *Start with Why*. The heart of his argument is that people will propel any *how* if they have a *why* to go with it. He depicts the relationships between purpose (why), methods (how), and product (what), and it begins with *why* in the middle. This clarity and sense of purpose provide the rocket fuel of dynamic action.

Put another way, my longtime friend and world-class entrepreneur Tom Suddes used to ask, "What do you want to be best at in the world?" This is not a rhetorical or esoteric discussion. Too often, people roll their eyes when you talk about mission and vision because they conjure up wasted hours of talk followed by a run-on paragraph tucked away in a report that no one will ever see again, let alone act upon.

Clarity matters. Knowing what you are about, why you are doing what you are doing, and measuring progress toward your goals are at the center of any successful enterprise, whether it is teaching, acting as an administrator, or in business as an employee or CEO. At Battelle for Kids, our work was crystal clear early on as we introduced value-added data to school district leaders. We helped them understand how it could be used as a lever to improve student performance. Timing was certainly part of our success. There was a gold rush and we were selling shovels. But you had to know how to use them, and you had to want to do it. Then federal legislation and subsequent state legislation made a useful tool into a required one. (When I think of successful business enterprises, I often wonder about the timing. Innovation needs to come along with an appetite for it.) Keep in mind that our big bet as a new organization was that we could improve student achievement in Ohio. That was our *why*. You must have a clear value proposition for your organization and think about the change you want and strategies to get it. Successful change on the ground includes constant communication, unrelenting pursuit, and support from multiple partners who advocate with you. The latter became easier for us once people saw the practical value of value-added data.

There's a training video I used to use in seminars that showed a team of basketball players making passes. I'd ask the audience to count the number of passes they saw, and afterward their answers came quickly: "29!" "27!" "31!" Then I asked, "Anybody see anything unusual?" In the middle of the film, a man comes out dressed in a gorilla suit, pounds on his chest, and leaves. But most people simply don't see it. I didn't see it the first time either. Why? Focus. We see what we look for. When I buy a white car, I suddenly see all the other white cars.

There are competing tensions in operating any entity; your greatest assets are your greatest assets until they are not. Patience is a wonderful attribute until quick, decisive action is needed. Decisive action is a wonderful attribute until more thoughtful approaches are needed. The same goes for focus. Focus usually provides a clear path forward, but sometimes flexibility is what's needed. The old adage "Keep your eye on the prize" works until it doesn't. Laser focus doesn't always serve you or the organization well. It's why we need others who focus on other things, especially danger signs ahead or, as I prefer, opportunities that may be tangentially related to your focus. The tension is always there between focus and flexibility, and good leaders know how to balance the two. Call it strategic flexibility. You need to stay aware of where you are and pull back when necessary or simply say no to some opportunities.

Customer Relationships

Relationships matter most in working with students and teachers and parents and, well, anyone and everyone. Customer relationships are no exception. Chances are your organization isn't the only one delivering your product or service. If you are first to the space, you have an early edge. But you will soon be followed by other competitors. It's what makes us all better. When that happens, customers have a choice. Why choose you? At Battelle for Kids, especially early on, if people wanted value-added data, they came to us because we were first in that training space and we partnered with the best analytic company in the world. Think about where you eat, shop, buy your cars, or do your dry cleaning. Is it always because you think they are the best in the world? Perhaps. But I suspect what keeps you coming back is a relationship. Someone at that organization sells their value to you personally. You like them. They are easy to work with. They smile, offer ideas, and empathize. And when they don't, we never forget it.

I'll never forget when my father was having surgery for lung cancer in May 1973. I was twenty-two years old and sitting alone, and an experienced and well-regarded surgeon came out to meet with me. He said, "Your father was filled with cancer, so I closed him up. There is no hope and he will die in four to six weeks." That was it. He was right, of course, but I sat stunned not only because of the news, but also the insensitive way it was delivered. I didn't need him to hold my hand, but how about thirty seconds of empathy that started with, "I'm sorry"? Physician training has come a long way, and this older doctor was probably a product of his time. But we changed all that because it matters. Bedside manner has an important place in caregiving.

So how do sellers, be they teachers or car salesmen or surgeons, build a relationship with buyers? For many, it's intuitive. They naturally know how to be interested rather than interesting. They ask questions, get feedback, and suggest ways to help. They always follow up and find ways to show appreciation. But that isn't true for everyone. Some staff members need someone to show them how to build relationships: practice by role playing and giving real feedback to get better. Just telling someone that you need to be "good with people" isn't enough. Some need ideas and concrete plans to do that. But they have to do it in their own authentic way.

I remember watching—painfully, I might add—as a very public official addressed crowds. She usually read her speeches, which often came across as cold and impersonal. Then she got a speech coach. Worse yet. Now, she would speak with crib notes, raising her hand for emphasis after reading a note that said, *raise hand for emphasis*. There was nothing authentic or persuasive about her remarks. And yet, on occasion, usually when the group was smaller and she spoke off the cuff, her remarks were authentic and sincere. She was being herself and it came through to the audience. She would have been so much better had she practiced and used these approaches with large groups. You can improve at any skill, including building relationships, but it has to be natural. If someone comes to see me with a checklist that includes asking me about my kids, that won't work.

Part of building relationships is communicating regularly: checking in with people or passing along articles or tips about topics you know they are interested in. Short texts or emails can make a difference. Get to know someone, pay attention to their needs, and find ways to help them. Think of the teachers you had who really cared about you, knew what you were interested in, and helped you find ways to fulfill your dreams. People remember these relationships all their lives.

One terrible example: I attended an awards event where the boss, who had been in the job nearly a year, tried to thank a longtime staffer who had coordinated the event, but could not remember his name. Now, we all have moments, but this was embarrassing. I felt bad for the staffer who had labored tirelessly for his boss and wasn't instantly known by the person he labored for! Many recognized the situation for what it was—at best, a missed opportunity to thank a deserving staff member, and at worst, a degrading moment for a boss who never paid enough attention to really know his staff, who was self-serving in his relationships and never the other way around.

And yet there is also that boss who years later can instantly recognize someone, recall a shared interest or something that person did when they worked together, and talk about it. Authentic relationship building is an ongoing process. It's knowing other people, asking about them, and creating a connection by showing a sincere interest in them. It's the opposite of the old joke: After talking incessantly about himself the narcissist finally said, "Enough about me. Let's talk about you. What do you think of me?"

Every individual relationship is important. The old adage, "You can count the seeds in an apple but not the apples in a seed" applies here. Once, I read a terrific editorial in *Education Week* that described exactly how I felt about the utility of using value-added assessment. The piece was brilliantly written by a college professor at Penn. I called him, congratulated him on the article, and told him a little about Battelle for Kids. We connected, and that call seeded a personal and professional friendship. A few years later he introduced us and our work to a school district that would become our largest client. One honest relationship. Not predicated on what you can do for me, but on what we share together.

Partnerships

Partnerships, of course, also begin with personal relationships, often bridged by a common interest. I used to describe the Battelle for Kids relationship with SAS, the largest privately held software company in the world, as a sort of peanut butter and jelly sandwich. They created world class metrics; we provided analytical training to understand the metrics; and we supported each other in our respective roles. It was good business for us both. When our state superintendent association lost a conference manager to retirement, I went to the executive director, a longtime friend and professional colleague, to see if we might fill that void and build a conference together. We did and it continued for another decade. But if a relationship opens this door, it is trust that propels it. And trust has to be built by experience with someone over time. I can't imagine a successful business staying successful over time without a cadre of trusting relationships and partnerships.

The key to partnerships is this: while you can do anything, you can't do everything. Find partnerships where you can both add value for your clients and, even better, do it seamlessly. That makes it a win-win.

Make it About Them

In the 1970s and '80s, most grant applications called for a needs assessment—a laundry list of items that you needed to be more effective. That terminology soon became pervasive. We asked people "what their needs were" prior to professional development activities. I banished that terminology at some point because it was vague and unclear. Sometimes people don't know what they need. Instead they often identify wants as needs. Ask people what their problems are. What are they struggling with? They can quickly tell you these, and therein lies what they need. Help people to find solutions to problems they identify. They just need to be asked.

The best selling experiences happen when you understand a customer's problem and talk through a possible solution. Too often, vendors offer a solution for a problem that was never identified. We have all seen organizations that have solutions in search of a problem. Or put another way, when your only tool is a hammer, everything is a nail! Selling is viewed negatively when you are pushing a good or service for a problem the buyer doesn't have. Make it about them, not you. Teachers who understand student strengths and weaknesses and can tailor their lessons to student needs and desires have a better chance of "selling" their services.

Then again, sometimes opportunities arise even if problems are not expressed, or people have completely different reactions to the same event. A true story is often told about twin boys raised by an alcoholic father. One boy followed in his father's footsteps and became an alcoholic too. The other became a teetotaler avoiding alcohol at all costs. Each attributes his behavior to what he experienced as a child. All of our experiences are filtered by how we see things, which influences us going forward. It's like another oft-told story of two shoe salesmen in Africa in the early 1900s. One telegraphs back, "Situation hopeless—they don't wear shoes." The other reports, "Glorious opportunity—they don't have shoes yet." The ultimate payback to you or your organization is more work, more trust, more good word of mouth. But it starts with them. When you help someone solve a problem, don't take credit for it. Let them take credit for it by being smart enough to work with you and use the tools you suggest. Eventually, credit will flow to you in the form of more opportunities to make an impact.

Here's another example. Two bright young staff members at Battelle for Kids worked with a superintendent to write a complicated grant in a short time, angling to partially solve a problem identified by his board. They collected data, met with staff, and prepared a concise executive summary and talking points for the board meeting. The result: home run! The board was delighted that the superintendent had acted so quickly, clearly, and expertly to move things along. Even better—they got the grant!

Now, the two staff members came to me mildly upset. Why? One said, "He used my words, my executive summary, and presented it to the board, who loved it. And did he mention me or my colleague or Battelle for Kids for jumping in to deliver all this in less than ten days? Of course not!" She added, "I think we should advertise our work and specific role in this project on our website."

I acknowledged the huge role they had played in this success, but asked, "Were you responsible for the entire board agenda, running the meeting, and implementing a gazillion other things? Did you have to meet with the press who was covering the meeting? Of course not. Did you help him start to solve a big problem? Of course you did. But it's not about you. You helped the customer look great and start to make a dent in their problem." They understood, but they were still miffed about the lack of credit. I assured them they would get credit, but it would not come in the public form they wanted.

Did the credit come? Absolutely—and in the way I wanted it. When the district received the grant, the superintendent quickly called me to ask, "Can you help us implement this?"

"Of course," I answered. I inquired about the work of our staff, which he said was just terrific. I then asked if he would privately drop each of them a quick personal note, as they would appreciate the positive reinforcement from him. Sure enough, in a week or so one of the staff members came to me with the note. "See," I said, "he did appreciate it but has a lot on his plate. And he specifically asked me to send you to help implement the grant. It's just not about us. It's about them and helping them be successful with myriad other confusing and complex pieces on their plate." There is another lesson worth repeating here. Credit does matter, and figuring out ways to acknowledge people for their work really, really matters. It is such a powerful motivator and takes so little to do it.

Making it "about them" works in other ways too. I once met a central office administrator from a large city district who told me about a human capital initiative that was working for them. I followed up later with a phone call, learned a lot, and asked if we might suggest other clients to visit them. When visiting a successful site, we often forget the benefit to the host: they make sure their program is good, check in with people, and get ready to put on a good show. Everyone benefits. I called again later, this time with a specific request. This district had received a large teacher effectiveness grant three years prior, and I wanted to chat about the lessons they'd learned, challenges, early successes, etc. People can talk easily and proudly of the things they do well. My chat was merely asking, listening, and learning. It was a great exchange and an opportunity to talk a little about our experiences in working with districts. Soon after, she called me to share a couple problems they were having, asked for our perspective, and ultimately our paid help. Always make it about them. In initial meetings, I think it is always better to allow the other party to talk about themselves. As Covey would say, "Seek to understand first."

> Pretend that every single person you meet
> has a sign around his or her neck that says, "Make
> me feel important." Not only will you succeed in
> sales, you will succeed in life.
> MARY KAY ASH

THE MAHONEY THREE

ONE: Randomly call some of your best stakeholders to gather feedback. For example, in a school you may call parents to get a sense of their children's experiences. In a business you may call some of your clients. The point is to gather feedback on a product or service they are using. It's a relationship call, not a sales call. You may also ask them to describe their biggest challenges at the moment. The latter helps you learn how you might help others in the future.

TWO: Create a scouting report and have team members visit organizations that have largely solved the challenges you are facing now. When I coached, I visited successful coaches to learn from them. As county superintendent, we organized teams to visit high-performing, high-poverty schools all over the nation. We came back and shared the results of successful leaders who faced our same problems.

THREE: Create an annual event for your best clients. Invite a speaker of common interest or distribute a helpful tool. Ask a couple clients to share a success story. Make the event short, appreciative, and useful to clients. You may choose to invite the CEO or a subset like communications directors, administrative assistants, etc. Just make the session relevant to them.

Chapter 21

CONTINUALLY IMPROVE

When you are through changing, you are through.
BRUCE BARTON

GOOD TEACHING IS ALL ABOUT continual improvement. You build on successes and adjust for flops. Each year you get a new group of students and a new beginning to try new things. You learn about new methods, get updated materials, and, through collaboration with other teachers, get new ideas and new models. Teachers are experts in adjusting and making changes.

The biggest room in any organization is the room for improvement. Change is driven by conditions as you see them now and as you would like them to be in the future. And that is always changing. Dynamic schools, businesses, and nonprofit organizations are constantly looking at research, technological advances, customer feedback, and data about student success rates, sales, and cost-benefit analyses. Responding to incoming information and feedback leads to continuous improvement, and that requires change.

We're watching a transformation of learning unfold as society grapples with COVID-19 and its after-effects, forcing us to explore new methods and ways to improve. When they were first introduced in schools in the mid-1980s, computers were transactional devices. We made them transformational as we found new ways for them to accomplish educational goals. As a college professor, I never wanted to teach online courses—not enough real time interaction, endless emails, and so on. Enter the coronavirus. Suddenly words that had no meaning to me in 2019 became part of my lexicon and practice in 2020: synchronous, asynchronous, Zoom, breakout rooms, and screen share are now part of my pedagogical transformation. At the center of this transformative era is learning and improving. I'm learning to teach differently with new tools, a new context, yet with some of the same old objectives. I still want to get to know my students, but I achieve that differently in the virtual space than in person.

Even as I write this, I'm wondering how the long-term impact of the pandemic on not just schooling but everything will force us to change and grow. The old rules don't apply. We are testing in real time whether people can be as productive working from home. Like most transformations, it may well be over before we realize what has been truly transformed in our lives. The old adage "Necessity is the mother of invention" has never been truer. It's a good thing I'm starting to like remote teaching, because I suspect we may never go back to some old ways of doing things. We have learned to do them differently because we had to. It's why I thank my teachers, parents, and others who gave me the most important tool in my life—a love of learning. When you are done learning and improving, you are done.

There are many forces that resist change in favor of the status quo. Many people are resistant to change; if you believe that your organization has reached its full potential, why would you change anything? But no organization I have ever been involved with—or even heard of—has maxed out their potential.

It is also tempting to make our efforts more about judgment than improvement. Bill Sanders's methodology that I embraced at Battelle for Kids was about improving, not simply judging. It's what you do with the information that matters: the idea was to have reliable student progress data that would help schools set goals and make changes to measurably help students. The No Child Left Behind Act ushered in an era of annual testing designed to hold schools accountable, and the Adequate Yearly Progress goals were supposed to push schools to continually improve. Evaluation, whether it be student performance, school performance, or sales performance, shouldn't be designed to prove, but rather improve.

Where a leader instills and insists on constant improvement, there is likely an organization getting better, outperforming others, and yes, having fun. Of course, improvement is not fairy dust that you sprinkle among employees. It begins with an attitude, followed by concrete actions to engage others, make plans, and execute them successfully.

Change

Change may be the most talked about, poorly practiced, and misunderstood leadership notion in the world. If a group pushes back on a half-assed idea, people say, "They can't handle change." No matter the quality of the idea, the expectations surrounding it, or its implementation—when it doesn't go well the answer is usually to blame those going through the change. Change is hard. Why would you want to do differently something that you understand and is comfortable for you? In *Influencer: The New Science of Leading Change*, Joseph Grenny suggests two critical questions for anyone attempting a substantive change. One, is the change worth it? If it isn't, why would you want to disrupt your work or life? (Put another way, the juice must be worth the squeeze.) Two, can you do what is expected? Again, if not, who will support the learning required? If leaders just thought through these two questions, we could dramatically calm some of the whitewater surrounding change.

Ever wonder why everyone is for change as long as they don't have to do anything different? It's always the other people who need changing. The truth is, you can't make people love change. You can help them feel less threatened by it, more supported in it, and to see the benefits from it. Think of a successful change you have led or been part of and why it worked. Now think of one that didn't work and why. That came quicker, didn't it? This isn't rocket science. When you ask people to share how a particular change was successful, they answer clearly. When you ask them to share how other efforts failed, they do that clearly as well. The two sets of answers make pretty good guideposts for leading through change.

We need to remember that change is always personal. I like the old adage that while not all change is progress, there cannot be progress without change. As a leader this is your job—to pursue and lead change successfully. It sure is easy for me to write about, but on the ground it is messy, imperfect, emotional, and, when completed, a thing of beauty. Failure is an orphan and victory has a thousand fathers. I often smile to see routine practices today that were born of real change and struggle—practices people didn't want changed until they had to be.

I always liked these three steps to change: initiating, implementing, and institutionalizing. Initiating says, "Let's get going." Implementing says, "Let's do something." And institutionalizing says, "It worked! Let's keep and expand it." But it begins with a leader whose belief system is open to the ideas of others, is not afraid to act and sometimes fail, and has the persistence to stay the course in spite of road bumps. An Irish pub I visited in Ennis had a sign: "Laziness may appear attractive, but work gives satisfaction." It does indeed from a leader who knows how to create and distribute it properly.

Initiating Change

In any organization under new leadership, change is in the air. It's usually a time to consider new goals and how to achieve them in the foreseeable landscape. Too often, school leaders allow the state to make testing the sole de facto goal. Yet there is so much more to educating children than test performance. It's an important goal but by no means the only one. It's also important to ask the community to assist in goal setting. After all, they own the buildings, and it's their children we are educating. Improvement is that space between where you are and where you want to be. If you want the community with you, they need to be part of the "where do you want to be" conversation. Let them help you establish a new vision.

Let me give a practical example. As middle school principal, I inherited a building that operated very much like a high school. Kids switched classes all over the building, went to lockers between class periods, kept track of their own stuff, and so on. There had to be a better way. I briefly considered changing the entire schedule, but large-scale change imposed is usually opposed. Instead I resolved to design and implement a new system for the following year. We embarked on a process that year involving staff, community, and students to create a new plan that would better meet the needs of students. We spent time outlining the process, including visits to other schools, community goal setting, faculty discussion, and so on, so everyone could see that we were working toward clarity around our goals for students. Then we could follow up with the best plan of organization to achieve those goals.

We had answered the two questions: the change was worth it, and we could do what was expected. We implemented our new plan the next year with widespread support. But did it work? Well, just a year after implementation, the school was selected as a blue-ribbon school by the US Department of Education and honored in a White House ceremony.

As a superintendent, I also worked to engage the community in initiating change. We created an eighteen-month strategic planning process for our district called "Charting the Course." We collected information on where we were, where we wanted to be, and how we would get there. It was our opportunity to think about what the future held for our children and what tools and programs would successfully prepare them for it. We created a video to highlight our proud history, the importance of planning forward, and how each person in the community might contribute to the process, and we showed it widely throughout the community to build momentum at the start. (A young primary student at one of these showings insisted that his mother must stay for the video when she clearly wanted to leave. He told her, "It's called Charlie the Horse!" For many months we laughed whenever we started a session with our *Charlie the Horse* video.)

We spent months figuring out a process to engage the community. The process is as important as the outcome, but outcomes matter. Don't become so mesmerized with the process that you forget the purpose. We completed our roadmap with specific, measurable goals for major operations in our district to benefit students. One of my early lessons on collaboration was this: even with a good process, you still need to worry about the outcomes. When you lead people down a particular path, they feel their time is wasted if there are no outcomes.

Our process included data collection of many sorts, from the physical status of our buildings to a telephone survey of residents. Many community meetings were held with the board and a board-appointed planning group to outline our goals for curriculum, instruction, facilities, transportation, and other key areas. Benchmarks were created to monitor progress.

A couple of important side notes here. If you are going to involve people in real change, make sure you are committed to doing it. Nothing is more deflating for people than to get behind something that never happens. But also clarify the process so you aren't creating unrealistic demands or setting yourself up for conflict. The second note is to ensure that the people who execute the plans are part of the planning process. Seems simple, but I can't tell you how many times the very people who must do the work are left out. And while nothing is impossible for those who don't have to do the work, no real progress is ever made without the people who do! Improvement, especially on a large scale, is a very large team sport!

Implementing Change

At Battelle for Kids, the districts we identified for value-added implementation were willing participants who shared our commitment to improvement. I met personally with each superintendent to make sure they knew what they were signing up for in the foreseeable future. It certainly helped that I knew almost all of them; relationships matter any time you are trying to move a new idea forward. People have to know and trust the messenger and believe in what you are selling. This was a pilot program. We were still testing whether our idea would prove true. But like me, they all believed in the idea because current measures were simply insufficient to motivate students and determine performance.

I was surprised by the number of high-performing districts that readily agreed to be part of our pilot project. After all, they were "winners" in the current system; these wealthy communities always produced high test results. But their attitude was expressed by one superintendent's comment: "Jim, we get great kids who do well in school. But I want to know if we are adding value and not simply being the recipient of great kids whose families support us." He wanted to know if he was lucky or leading. He understood that the SAS value-added data wasn't simply a tool to give low performers a chance to show progress more easily (a common misconception was the lower the past performance, the easier it was to show gain). The sophisticated calculation measured a student's past performance, made a projection about where they were likely to score, and then compared that projection to the observed score to determine gain.

I could go back to Doug Reeves's four quadrants: Lucky (high achievement, little progress), Losing (low achievement, low progress), Learning (low achievement, high progress), Leading (high achievement, high progress). We had overwhelming evidence that students in high-achieving districts could make progress, and yes, there were kids in low-achieving schools who made no progress. I have often said that the dirty little secret in education is that your status as an educator often comes from the status of the community. If you work in an affluent suburb, your status is different than if you work in a poor Appalachian community like the one I worked in. But your status should come not from who you teach, but what you do with those you teach. I still believe that, and value-added data was a partial measure of our effectiveness in working with any group of children.

There were some things we did right—consciously and unconsciously. First, let me start with the obvious. We believed in the change we were promoting, and then sold it. We got other people to believe in it, too, and to partner with us. So, we had a pilot group of believers, a world-class statistician, and a company to do the metrics. We enlisted others who could propel our work. Then I worked to involve groups who otherwise might dislodge us.

The first formidable group of dislodgers I was worried about was the professorial class, especially statisticians in higher education. I didn't want district leaders out there making assumptions, reviewing data, and taking action, only to have some group of highly educated math folks say they weren't practicing sound science and their conclusions were bogus. Or, "Why would we have SAS calculate these when we have universities in Ohio that could do this?" I arranged for Dr. Sanders to meet with university deans, and I invited higher education folks to regional gatherings and statewide meetings. These meetings proved to be invaluable as Bill mesmerized professors with his methodology and years of research, enlisting them in our movement. They saw the research and learning opportunities our work presented.

Other potential dislodgers were Ohio's teacher unions. Our goal was to put metrics in place to enlighten and improve educator efforts; of course there was pushback, as you could foresee the potential for teacher evaluation, performance pay, and accountability emanating from this new metric. I'd like to say that never happened, and some would say I reneged on my promise to not do that. We didn't renege on our promise, but every innovation has a dark side. I remember telling union leaders in New York City, "Look, there are a lot of bad things you can get on the internet, but that's not an argument for disbanding the internet. You must advocate for the highest and best uses of data." I regularly shared our continuing efforts with union leadership, because you won't accomplish anything by alienating your entire workforce! I had been a strong supporter of the teacher union as a teacher. You can't spend all your time with folks who can derail your work, but there are often key constituencies for whom a little communication and understanding goes a long way. And if their complaints can't be mitigated, you at least know all the counterarguments.

The energy for implementing change is around champions—those who share your vision for the promise of a new practice or innovation. In our case, we had supportive associations of superintendents, school board members, and the five major state business associations. The best strategy is to talk with people about the innovation—its benefits, obstacles, and how they might help. Talk to people again. And again. Building relationships and understanding takes time. As we thought about how to institutionalize the use of value-added assessment across Ohio, we outlined key people and groups to have conversations with and became laser focused on the value of value-added.

A lobbyist once offered me this valuable tidbit of advice: "If someday you hope to have legislation requiring the use of value-added, you might want to include districts where key legislators live. Whatever you're looking for in a district, this should be a factor too." Simple, yet brilliant. He went on, "I've learned that groups in the state capital can lobby for all kinds of things, but when legislators hear the same messages from people back home, it really matters." This was truly sage advice and long-term thinking.

Making Successful Change

In the '90s I used a simulation game in my graduate classes called Making Change Happen. The goal was to create more equity for students in a make-believe school district. Teams of four to six players were given demographic descriptions of a district, a game board, and people cards representing board members, administrators, teachers, parents, and others in the district, with a short description of each person and some insights into their experiences and philosophy. Players could "purchase" a diagnosis of the district outlining past efforts at improving equity and social information, such as who knows who and how (in other words, relationships between and among key players). Each team made a number of strategic moves; just like real life, the consequences differed. The goal was to earn "stubens," a currency awarded when your district successfully made changes that benefited students. The first time I played the game, I was totally taken with it. It was crystal clear that whoever had developed the game understood the school context, how successful change was made, and the critical roles various people play. I used the lessons I learned in that game to help lead Battelle for Kids a decade later. Players always laughed during the debrief because they readily understood how successful teams generated more stubens. What are those lessons of successful change?

First, successful change is not about converting staff. I have witnessed in practice and in the game people's persistence in trying to convert staff to their point of view. Isn't that what you are supposed to do? No. The objective of the game (or any change in schools) is to benefit students, not to convert staff. I have seen this failure repeated many times over.

Second, know your end result. During the last decade, Battelle for Kids worked with many districts across the country to implement a variation of merit pay for teachers. Too often leaders, particularly from the business sector, saw merit pay as the silver bullet. Simply pay people more for better results. Makes sense, doesn't it? Where those results can be easily and consistently measured, it does work at times. But I've seen leaders become so enamored by the sexiness and publicity of the change that they forgot to ask, "How will this help kids?" I support teachers making more money, but it is naïve to think paying them more will automatically result in increased student benefits. The question I always lead with to the person in charge is, "If your change were implemented successfully, what would be different for students?"

Another example is the proliferation of technology across the country. Many schools provide students with iPads or computers. Some leaders become so jazzed by all the things technology can do, they forget what kids can do. They forget that technology is just a tool to enhance learning, not the whole enchilada. Getting kids the technology is just part of the change, not the end result. Most car dealerships are terrible about this. After the tech whiz talks nonstop for thirty minutes about the new car's features they ask, "Any questions?" Are you kidding me? I'm so overwhelmed, I'm just glad I know how to put the car in gear and drive home.

Imagine if the person had led with a question like, "What technology do you currently use in your old car that you want in the new one?" I would say, "I want to use Bluetooth to do hands-free calling." Start there. A good idea poorly implemented is the same as a bad idea implemented well. Neither work. But enough of my bird walk about change.

Institutionalizing Change

Making Change Happen also teaches lessons on institutionalizing change. Perhaps the most important is that administrative support and approval is needed for the change to occur. A teacher needs the principal to stand behind classroom changes; the principal needs the superintendent's support for major building changes; the superintendent needs the school board's support for district changes; and, ultimately, elected school board members need the support of the community.

Consider the scale, enormity, and impact of the change you are considering. Sometimes it is a waste of time to get approval for something you can and perhaps should do. The superintendent doesn't need to know that you have changed class rotation times for second graders to take art, music, and PE. But if you are considering eliminating social studies in the primary grades to double up on reading instruction, that probably needs to be discussed with the superintendent. What is the decision-making calculus on all this? I could provide a rubric, and some would use it as an exact guide. But there isn't an exact guide. This is where judgment comes in handy. As a leader, you have to be connected enough to the staff to know what response a change is likely to draw from them, and connected enough to your boss to know what issues require a thorough discussion. If you are closing a school building, that is likely a big issue for the community. Painting the hallways in school colors probably isn't one, unless you are taking pictures down.

Institutionalizing change requires administrative support, but it also requires buy-in from the staff. You would be surprised at how often a leader misdiagnoses a situation and applies a solution that does more damage by attempting to solve a problem others never saw. Reasonable people can disagree on the solution, but it helps if they agree on the problem they are trying to solve. Rather than subjecting everyone all at once to a change, go to those who already support the change and develop a critical mass of support. Suppose, as a principal, you have a team of teachers who want to implement a proven strategy to improve reading comprehension or try a different approach to classroom management. Before you expect the entire staff to implement the idea, why not encourage this small band of teachers to try it, regularly monitor their progress, share it with the rest of the staff, and let it unfold. Again, the goal isn't to convert staff. It's to help students. If these teachers see student benefits, they will do more of it, share their enthusiasm with others, and the movement will grow without the need for heavy-handedness. You want it to be their idea.

This brings me to another point about change in general and leadership in particular. Nobody wants to play in a band where the leader gets all the solos and, even worse, hogs the credit! Empower people with authority, autonomy, and responsibility. Giving others credit for success only strengthens the change and ultimately helps the leader. Watch the pronouns people use. *I* and *me* need to be replaced often with *we* and *our*. An interesting study reviewed the effects of narcissistic CEOs on company performance. It turned out the more *I*'s the CEO uses in their annual letter to stockholders, the more likely the company performance is to be poor or erratic.

A final lesson from the game: it takes time and persistence, especially with the thorny issues that involve a lot of people. Some practices can and should be changed in a moment (banning certain clothing items as part of the dress code) while others will take longer (equity in school funding).

But you have to start. Some people find it abhorrent to accept half a loaf in change, especially for complex problems. I don't. If you continue to move the needle, you eventually have the whole loaf. If you refuse to accept anything but the entire loaf, you risk losing it all and gaining nothing. Your job is to lead change. Find the things that matter to students. Build support. Initiate. Implement. Institutionalize.

THE MAHONEY THREE

ONE: Ask your staff to describe their best and worst experience implementing a new change. Share results in small groups, identifying common themes for successful and unsuccessful changes. This exercise reveals in practical terms why some changes work and others don't. It's a primer for your own efforts brought to you by your own staff.

TWO: Here is a way to make people "feel change." Ask two people to stand back to back. Assign one to be the teacher and one the student. Direct the teacher to change five things about themselves in ninety seconds with no other instruction. Then have them turn around and see if the student can identify the changes. Then ask the teacher to change ten things in three minutes. People will quickly groan, and you can stop. How did you feel? What are the applications to learning and change? What kinds of changes did people make? Are these the only ones that count?

THREE: Ask leaders to rank their employees' performance, listing their names vertically on a piece of paper with the highest performers at the top. Next to that list, rank the same people based on how much time the leaders spend with them each week. Draw lines connecting the two lists: Connect Bob to Bob, Sara to Sara, etc. What do the lines tell you? Do they connect directly or cross over? It's a visual catalyst for discussion about the leader's time and employee performance. With whom do they—or should they—spend the most time?

Chapter 22

THERE'S NO LEADERSHIP WITHOUT FOLLOWERSHIP

Leadership is getting other people to do what you want them to do because they want to do it.
DWIGHT D. EISENHOWER

EVER SEE A TURTLE ON A FENCE POST? That old saying really points out the fact that few of us ever to get anywhere without someone helping us along the way. There is no leadership without followership. And followership must be seeded, cultivated, and nurtured. When it is done well, you all grow. Looking back, any achievements associated with me were the result of others sharing a similar vision, working tirelessly together, and sometimes—not enough—celebrating our success. Too often we barely finish one thing before we are on to the next. The joke in education, too often the truth, is that whatever you do becomes the "first annual," and you rarely if ever drop something.

Great leaders don't bully others into submission. They inspire others to follow them by having a clear vision, engaging multiple partners, and replacing *I* with *we*. Without followership there is only power and formal authority. Compliance may give the appearance of followership, but it is usually disengaged. How much does disengagement cost? Gallup estimates that well over 50 percent of the workforce is disengaged at work, translating to approximately $7 trillion in lost productivity. What is particularly harmful is the opportunities that are lost because people aren't connecting; they're just keeping their heads down. What does disengagement look like? People do their job at the minimum level to keep it. Initiative dies. Collaboration withers. Communication is nonexistent. People in this state have lost their zest for improving the company's mission, impact, or bottom line. They have been put in their place and now offer their bare minimum.

How does this occur? When people feel left out. Their ideas aren't heard. They don't trust people they work with. Then they complain and bring others down with them. You sometimes see it in a teacher's lounge when someone decries anything done by an administrator to anyone who will listen. Disengaged folks are unhappy and want others to join them.

Great leaders inspire others to follow them. It's an interactive process between both parties—leaders create followers. It's why some teachers will forgo financial incentives but will follow a great principal to another school. Or why customers will follow a good butcher, car salesman, or hairdresser. They harness loyalty.

Simon Sinek argues that there are only two ways leaders can create followership: either inspire it or manipulate it. Manipulations include price, novelty, promotions, or even fear. After 9/11, Southwest Airlines sent $1,000 vouchers to its best customers. Or two-for-one sales. Or free T-shirts to the first five thousand attendees at a ballpark. Marketing messages are used because they work. Inspiration, though, taps into the *why* of motivation. The *why* is your purpose, what gets you out of bed in the morning and taps into your higher calling. It's the feeling we have when those around us share common beliefs and values. It's why people will wait six months to get a Harley-Davidson motorcycle or pay more for an Apple computer.

Great leaders hire those who share their beliefs about the organization's mission. Herb Kelleher, founder of Southwest Airlines, famously said, "You don't hire for skills. You hire for the right attitude. You can always teach skills." Trust is built when followers believe that leaders are driven by more than self-gain. It isn't about holding the highest rank. They follow you because they want to. You have indeed tapped into their *why*.

Leadership Troubles

Perhaps the most insidious folks I've seen are those described as "kiss up and kick down" leaders (or worse: "kiss up and piss down"), usually mid- to upper managers who work very hard to please superiors and treat those below them just the opposite. At lower levels they criticize subordinates, blame others for mistakes, and take credit for anything done right. This group is particularly dangerous because their superiors are often hoodwinked by their efforts to ingratiate themselves with the boss. At upper levels these folks are liked because they appear to get things done, are personally and professionally affirming to bosses, and often have great skills. But their tactics drive subordinates away to other jobs or make them disengaged. I've had this experience myself. I once hired a highly qualified person—degrees from prestigious universities, experience at top-tier companies, and a warm personality. It was six months before their subordinates finally reported the lack of teamwork, micromanagement, and blame for missed deadlines or average product. Often by the time upper management figures it out, the damage has been done.

Let's look at a hypothetical scenario. Mike the CEO asks his employee Jane how things are going on her team. Jane replies honestly, "Actually, we are all struggling a little bit with Harold. He is so knowledgeable and cares deeply about what we do, but sometimes he doesn't trust us to get things done."

Mike asks, "Have you or other team members talked to Harold about your concerns?"

"Well," Jane says, "we have tried, but he gets defensive and seems to question our loyalty."

Instead of taking Jane's remarks seriously, Mike dismisses them as sour grapes. He says, "Thanks for sharing—but we need you to get along with Harold." And the cycle continues. Why? The boss doesn't want to undercut the person they've hired and, frankly, employees are often displeased with a new boss, especially one who is successful. Mike chalks it up to several possibilities but rarely to the possibility that the person he has hired is a destructive force.

Eventually Mike hears the same story from others, sees talented people leave, and figures it out. Sometimes not. Harold may maintain his position by hiring loyal, compliant folks who are happy to be told what to do and rarely exercise creativity, autonomy, or their own leadership. If a leader suspects they have a Harold in their organization, they should get input from others and figure out what is going on before the situation worsens.

Could this entire scenario have played out differently? Yes. What if a transparent evaluation system enabled everyone to share their views about others, especially bosses? Think of it as a kind of early warning system that enables honesty, new expectations, and adjustment. Personnel problems are always messy, but you can implement systems that promote honest feedback and the opportunity for changes in behavior.

Leaders need to know something about the field in which they lead. The notion that leadership skills can be easily transferred from one field to another is nonsense. Could an effective business leader readily transfer their skills to become a rifle company commander in the US Army? Could a popular and great leader for a large library system become a hospital administrator? In some cases yes, but not without serious devotion to understanding the business they are now leading. Sometimes it takes a lifetime of experiences to build the intuitive knowledge required to lead in a particular field.

What kind of leader are you? I kept a placard in my office for years that simply said, "All people bring happiness. Some by coming, others by leaving." Social psychologists know that just being near someone in a good mood can boost performance, and grumpiness has the opposite impact. We sync up with the emotional state of those who lead us. Let's be honest here. We all have moments—bad weather days, if you will, or quick storms, but when they become patterns in a consistent climate of negativity, that's a problem.

Symbolic Leadership

How leaders spend their time symbolizes what they truly value. Time spent connecting with and celebrating others speaks volumes. One of the things I liked most about the superintendency was the chance to seed ideas, thank people, and influence direction. All these approaches become part of the culture, or "the way we do things around here." Others take their cues from what you talk about, participate in, and pay attention to—in sum, from what and how you choose to spend your biggest asset: time. And it's not just the big things but the little things. Going to less popular sporting events like a junior high volleyball game says you care about all athletes; visiting a bus driver in the hospital says you care about operations staff; sending birthday cards says everyone matters. But there is a caution here: these things must be done authentically.

I had a colleague who had his secretary mail birthday cards to each employee on their birthday. I was with him when we went through the lunch line and a cook thanked him for her card. It was obvious to both the cook and me that he had no idea what it was for, and her expression went from genuine thanks to disgust. Symbolically, this was a failure. Alternatively, for years on each Friday I had my secretary list whose birthday was coming up the next week. I would then write a short personal note to each person. When I left one person said, "You are the only one who remembered my birthday every year, and I will miss those cards and notes." Your organization may be too large to make this practical, but figure out a way to show that people matter using small personal recognitions.

Another favorite practice of mine was to call a dozen or so parents throughout the year about their child's experiences at school. I'd learn a little about each child from their schedule or participation in various clubs, etc., then call the parent. These calls were unexpected, of course, but often revealing, and I'm certain they were shared with others. Symbolic leadership is not about what you do as much as what it means for others. Riding one school bus route communicates volumes to the bus garage and parents who have to put children on buses at 6:15 each morning. Let's be honest: you don't have to drink a gallon of milk to know it's spoiled. A simple experience can uncover a practice that just doesn't make sense or has lost its value.

One of the most powerful symbolic opportunities is giving an introduction or making a few comments at a meeting. This is your chance not just to communicate but to connect with a group, to let them know that you know how they feel, understand their challenges, or appreciate their efforts. One March I was asked to speak at the quarterly meeting of our local ministers' group, composed of ministers from places of worship across the district. I wanted to connect with them and answer their questions; after all, in rural areas like ours people often hear false rumors about schools that I don't even know about! We had missed many days of school in January and February, and now it looked as if spring break might be canceled in April to make days up. One minister asked, "Is it true that spring break isn't going to be used for makeup days because area superintendents all have a cruise planned for those dates?"

I about choked, but I appreciated the question. "No," I said, "but I sure wish I was going on a cruise!" I assured them that superintendents would never make decisions for hundreds of staff and thousands of students based on their personal plans, and they didn't have to be in the district if school was in session. If I hadn't agreed to speak at the meeting, I would've missed the opportunity to answer this question.

Celebrations are also a tool of symbolic leadership. Don't just wait for natural celebrations like graduations. Invent some. In our district we wanted all high school students to participate in at least one extracurricular activity. To do that we needed teachers and adult supervisors. So while we honored our coaches in the fall as part of National Coaches Day, we created a spring event to honor our extracurricular advisors, from those who directed the yearbook to those who organized and advised a small club. It might be a breakfast where we would have a handful of students, especially recent graduates, share how those experiences had meant so much to them. We often had past participants write letters to advisors to compile in a small book. These events remind advisors of their importance, keep them advising, and make celebration part of your culture.

Ask yourself this question: what do you want your classroom, building, district, or agency to be known for? And then a year later, ten years later, if you were put on trial for doing or not doing that, what evidence would you present? I just can't say enough about small things done well over time. They have a cumulative impact, just like erosion will wear away rock over time, and cathedrals are built brick by brick. Start. Now.

Ownership

I learned as a social studies teacher that while we studied American history, we learned our best lessons by studying local events. American history is local history. It is said that just after the attack on Pearl Harbor, FDR told Senate Appropriations Chair Kenneth McKellar, "I have an extraordinary request. The Germans are building a bomb that could destroy the world. We need to beat them to the task. I need you to hide a billion dollars in the appropriations for this highly secretive project. No one can know of our intentions. Can I count on you?"

McKellar, a Tennessee native, leaned in close to the President and said, "Of course you can count on me. I just have one question. Where in Tennessee do you wish to build this facility?" Thus began the Manhattan Project, which transformed pastureland in Oak Ridge, Tennessee, into a bustling city in just eighteen months. Former Speaker of the House Tip O'Neill was right when he noted all politics is local.

Leadership is local too. At the local level you own it. They know you. A state superintendent once told me that they had to be accountable for results at the state level and that the same should be true at the local level. I retorted, "In local communities we have much more than accountability. We have ownership. You can go to a grocery store after a state board meeting and no one knows who you are. Real accountability is when you go to the grocery store and people ask why you hired a particular coach, why you need more tax money, why you don't use diesel fuel in buses to save money, and on and on. Ownership is personal," I continued, "because you know them, and they know you." It's not simply metrics.

Part of ownership is understanding yourself: knowing what you stand for or against, who you are, and what people can expect from you. You have to put those things first. There's an exercise where small groups are given three large rocks, gravel, sand, and water, and they must fit all these items into a fishbowl. There is a trick. Unless you put the three rocks in first, the other ingredients won't fit. The big rocks are a metaphor for who you are and what you stand for—your values, if you will. It's the big things in your life. When you live by your values, trust ensues. A kindergarten teacher once brought me a note from a parent that read, "Dear Mrs. P., Janie said she needed a note for something today. Here it is. Signed, Mrs. M." We both laughed, but think about what this note represented: trust to the highest degree. The mother wrote a blank trust check to the school because of the kindergarten teacher. Your big rocks as a leader are important. They tell everyone who you are and what you stand for in good or troubled times.

Context of Leadership

Accountability is not simply about metrics. Real accountability involves ownership—ownership of your vision and values, your decisions, and your outcomes. I've often been struck by similarities and differences between education and business leaders beyond the different context in which each provides leadership. There is a widespread opinion that if school systems were run more like businesses, they would be more successful. Underpinning this theory is the belief that business leaders are more decisive, tolerate less subpar performance, and set measurable goals. But simply saying "let's run schools like businesses" ignores the complexities of ownership by leaders in the public sphere.

Furthermore, if a business operated like a school, it would soon be out of business. I would never paint any group with the same brush, but here are a couple of real examples. I had the opportunity to meet with a global business CEO who was getting ready to retire. He had a sincere interest in school improvement, and he thought his business could develop a training program that would be successful in a school setting, using the same principles they used to train their associates. Retired associates from this top international firm would serve as mentors, offering counsel, business tools, and ideas to support the principals. He wanted to partner with our organization to launch this program. So far, so good.

I suggested that he come to Columbus and I would gather ten of the brightest educators in the room who understood schools and the principal-ship role, had multiple successful leadership experiences, and would listen to his proposal. We knew schools and the complicated social architecture that accompanied new principals, and we'd provide feedback on his proposal from a practitioner's view.

I asked, "What if we don't like it or think it won't work?"

He sincerely replied, "Then I will accept that but respectfully ask for ways to make it work." His response was both clear and honest and I looked forward to his visit.

He arrived early on a Monday morning to make his presentation. But I had a question before he began. "With complete respect," I asked, "I'm won-dering, if I met with you at your headquarters in New York, how might you react if I suggested that we could improve your associates' performance using great retired school principals as mentors and a training program aimed at their level of consulting?" There was an audible silence in the room. I simply wanted him to feel for a moment what it felt like to be one of us.

He didn't hesitate. "I'd like to think that meeting could have been scheduled and I would have listened to all your ideas for improvement," he replied with sincerity and humility that we all believed in that moment. Do I think most CEOs would have responded that way? I doubt it. He was truly a unique business leader who genuinely cared about school improve-ment. He could have spent his retirement doing anything he wanted, and he wanted to make a difference in schools. We had a great discussion and eventually assembled a large team of educators and business folks to cre-ate a relevant curriculum. But we were never successful in generating true business-educator partnerships to implement this program on a wide scale. On a personal note, though, I never respected a CEO more as he continued his work improving schools.

The truth is that school superintendents operate in a public setting that requires a combination of business, political, and social acumen. If business directors were publicly elected and their board meetings and agenda were open to the public, the decision-making calculus would change. It's simply a different context and goals are not the same, so the refrain "run it like a business" falls flat.

A retired CEO once teased me about whether our mutual friend might be interested in a large city superintendency. I laughed and said, "Probably too late for him at this stage of retirement!" I added, though, "Given the size and complexity of this role, I think the pay should be more commensurate with the private sector."

"I agree," he said. "There would be much better candidates."

His quick response belies a common belief that if we paid more, we would get better candidates. Perhaps. But not everybody, and not all great leaders, are motivated by compensation. If so, we could improve military, fire department, police department, and government service by adding dollars to paychecks. There are fortunately people, very capable ones, who still want to serve the public in ways that make a difference in the lives of others. Daniel Pink's motivators—purpose, autonomy, and mastery—apply to leaders as much as they do to any employee.

Yes, it can be lonely at the top. Without followers, it is incredibly lonely. There may be times when you feel as though you are leading the charge and no one is behind you. Great leadership involves developing and maintaining relationships, sharing the purpose, respecting autonomy, and appreciating others' contributions. It's a mistake to characterize any profession's leadership with a one-size-fits-all judgment. I suspect that great leaders who produce results, care about people, and know how to lead are pretty evenly distributed across all professions. And so are the bad ones.

THE MAHONEY THREE

ONE: Create your own survey to distribute to groups you supervise or impact. Use the feedback to support followers, ensure organizational alignment, and solidify approaches to challenges. Do it regularly, formally and informally, so you have a sense of what is going on in your organization.

TWO: Celebrate birthdays and more. Begin each Monday by having cards ready for those who will have a birthday that week. Write a personal note not only about their birthday, but in acknowledgment of other things. If you see them, you will know to add greetings in person, and doing it yourself places that person in your mind. Don't delegate this.

THREE: Create an annual celebration of the organization's accomplishments and contributions of the staff. You might honor staff for their years of service, provide gifts to recognize committee workers, etc. Invite stakeholders to speak (parents, clients, etc.). Make it memorable.

Chapter 23

IF YOU CAN'T TEACH, YOU CAN'T LEAD

I touch the future. I teach.
CHRISTA MCAULIFFE

THE SKILLS I LEARNED as a teacher have been incredibly valuable to me in every position I have had. Leaders in any field would do well to think of themselves as teachers. Leadership ultimately is not about what you believe, but what you do—the actions you take to build strong teams, motivate others, develop relationships, and by extension build culture.

In the early 1990s, Ohio passed a law that started the journey to test-based accountability. Students were required to pass ninth-grade proficiency tests in math, English, science, and social studies to receive a high school diploma. As ninth graders got ready to take these exams for the first time, we were concerned that their last exposure to civics had been in the eighth grade. The principal decided to create a six-week civics refresher and to find a substitute qualified to teach the course.

Instead, I suggested that I could teach the classes. After all, I had taught the subject for seven years. We were concerned that I would get called out to handle other things, disrupting the classes. But I really wanted to do this, because I wanted to see if I could still teach kids. Or had I become so administrative that I'd forgotten how it feels to be a teacher? I also wanted to be responsible for how our students did on this first test. It's what I was asking of other teachers: teach a class, test the students, and make the results public. Pretty straightforward—and threatening.

Our middle school principal was also a former social studies teacher and agreed to teach half a day for six weeks. That way I wouldn't be tied up all day, and he and I could swap out mornings for afternoons if needed. I was a little afraid that this might look like a PR stunt, so we didn't publicize our efforts at all. This was serious work.

We were both nervous and excited as we began planning the course. We pored over objectives, strategies, and materials we might use. I suggested we order some materials from a testing company, and he looked at me and asked seriously, "You mean we can just order these?" I laughed and answered, "Yes, Jack, I'm the superintendent! I ought to be able to do a few things without a committee!" We laughed, ordered the materials, and got ready for the six weeks.

It turned out that kids were still kids. After two days they didn't have a clue that I was the district superintendent. I had to deal with behavior issues until students became accustomed to my style and expectations. It was a terrific experience, reminding me of the isolation of teachers in general, the hectic pace from period to period with little time to go to the restroom, and the responsibility for managing so many parts at once. We finished the six weeks, kids took the test, and we went back to our former roles.

I really enjoyed working with Jack, who had a great sense of humor and most of all was a real collaborator in planning and critiquing the classes we taught. Gallup again has it right with their Q12 survey, which emphasizes the importance of having a "best friend" at work. While folks have long raised brows about the question, Gallup's wording is intentional and research is clear: having a trusting, easy partner to plan, critique, and commiserate with has a positive impact on performance.

I remember the day the results came back. I quickly surveyed all the results, and then of course our specific ones from social studies. I called Jack immediately. "Jack, what were you doing on those afternoons in social studies? I thought you were following the same lesson plan as me."

"I was," he answered. "Why?"

"Well, I have the results. In the morning classes I taught, nearly all students passed, while in your classes…well, let's just say the scores were much, much worse. I'm not sure how I'm going to explain this."

He stammered, apologized, and offered excuses.

I couldn't hold my laughter any longer. I confessed, "I'm making it up. All of our kids did well in social studies and every other subject area. Congratulations. We can feel good about this!" Laughter cements relationships that matter to us.

This little exercise reminded me of what it means to be a teacher. Too often we become detached from the reality of the classroom. Worse yet, there is the crowd that believes leadership is leadership and that prerequisite experience as an educator doesn't matter. Seriously? Can you imagine a successful leader with no technical knowledge or experience in their field? Any leader would be wise to figure out how to go back and feel what it's like to work in that field. Make your own version of *Undercover Boss*.

Great Teaching and Great Leading Are the Same

You must be able to teach before you lead. Teaching is leading whether your class is a group of eighth graders, the staff and students of an entire school, or a country with three hundred and thirty million people. How you define and carry out your role makes all the difference. And you get to decide it. One year, our district was given limited tickets to a popular event, so we put limits on the number of tickets you could purchase to keep others from being shut out. I learned afterward that one administrator had bullied the secretary into selling him extra tickets. I confronted him, and his answer still rings with me: "Why wouldn't I ask for more? After all, there should be some privileges to leading!"

"There are," I countered, "but leadership also has responsibilities, and these should come first."

How you see your job determines how you do your job and how you behave in it. Leaders who want to ensure that staff behavior is consistent with the culture they are trying to build must model that behavior themselves.

In the early 2000s, a team at Battelle for Kids partnered with a University of Michigan business researcher, Robert Quinn, to study highly effective teachers from Texas, Ohio, and Tennessee. These teachers were remarkable people. Identified by their consistently high value-added scores, they took whatever kids were assigned to them each year to higher academic ground than similarly achieving students in other classrooms. Quinn's research found that effective CEOs have the same skills as effective teachers, including the ability to successfully integrate relationship building, goal setting, innovation, and consistent systems for quality, especially when these areas are at odds.

Good teaching is good leading. And good leading is good teaching. Highly effective teachers, like effective CEOs, are able to run complex organizations (classrooms) with a set of often competing values—goals versus relationship building and structure versus creativity. Great teachers and leaders integrate them successfully. The skill sets are strikingly similar, just applied to different audiences.

When I went into administration, I was looking for purpose, autonomy, and mastery. What I found was that I was still a teacher, but in a different setting. Teaching middle school social studies and coaching gave me the foundational experience I needed to be an administrator. School administration at its best is servant leadership and good teaching. Connect with your community, get to know the people, understand the challenges, show up and be present.

Let's flip the terrible adage, "Those who can, do, and those who can't, teach." Maybe it should be, "Those who can't teach, can't do." Instead of saying effective teachers are like effective leaders, how about acknowledging that successful leaders are like effective teachers? As a sports coach I was sometimes told that people like me got hired for coaching and not teaching. The logic was that you might be good at one and not the other. No. Good coaches are good teachers. Period. Each demands the ability to lead people to achieve common goals using skills, knowledge, and intuition. I saw it in 2018 just after the horrific school shooting in Parkland, Florida. A suburban superintendent in Columbus invited everyone to a public meeting to discuss school safety. He had the police chief there along with other service providers to share what they did and ask for ideas. He didn't assume his plans were good enough, nor was he waiting until a tragedy occurred before doubling down on safety considerations. He created a teachable moment. That is leading. He didn't wait until he was pressed to act on raw emotion, which can be tricky and often wrong. He knew people were concerned right then about what was happening in the country, and he took the opportunity to engage them in productive conversation.

Over the years, I've talked to many young people who aspired to become teachers but were dissuaded by their own teachers, parents who were successful in other fields, and college advisors. And yet all those people who were effective in other fields were great teachers, too. They knew how to motivate others, apply knowledge, create new approaches, and build relationships.

Think of the best teacher you ever had; I suspect they possessed all these attributes. But if I said, "Imagine a leader who motivates others, insists on goals, builds relationships, and innovates with new approaches. What's their field?" Most people won't say teaching. Try it. You'll get "coach," "businessperson," "policy maker," "president." And yet these are all teachers too, even if some abhor the thought of it. Why would they? Because we pay teachers less—a lot less in some cases. We think sometimes of the worst teachers rather than the best—we think of them as babysitters. Collectively we have created a cultural delusion in which we respect teachers less, hope our children don't become one, and forget that teachers are the corps that make all other professions possible.

If You Can't Teach, You Can't Lead

Imagine for a moment the best teacher you ever had. You decide what "best" means for you. For one person, it might be that teacher who taught you advanced mathematics so well that you easily passed introductory calculus in college. For another, it could be that teacher who offered emotional support through countless listening and advising sessions as you were struggling with home issues. For yet another, it could be that teacher who saw a talent in you and found opportunities for you to grow that turned out to be life changing. What makes someone "best" is often determined by what we need at the time, and looking backward we remember the teacher who gave it to us.

Now bring that person up in your mind. Did they engage you and have your attention? Did they expect much of you, hold you accountable, and maybe on more than one occasion irritate you because of those things? Did they know you, recognize your strengths, and encourage your participation? Did they acknowledge your achievements? Did they successfully lead you through change by encouraging you to try something new? Did their enthusiasm, empathy, or patience motivate you? My guess is that your answer to all or nearly all of these questions is a resounding YES. I've described what great teachers do. And of course, like all humans, your teachers did some of these things better than others, but they worked on all of them with you. They took an interest in your life and in your work. They nurtured and cared about you.

Now remember the best boss you ever had. Think about what that boss did to put them front and center for you. Again, it will be based on what "best" meant for you at the time. Did they engage you and have your attention? Did they expect much of you, hold you accountable, and on more than one occasion irritate you because of those things? Did they know you, recognize your strengths, and encourage your participation? Did they acknowledge your achievements? Did they successfully lead you through change by encouraging you to try something new? Did their enthusiasm, empathy, or patience motivate you? My guess is that once again your answer will mostly be a resounding YES.

And so it is that if you can't teach, you can't lead. Think of some of the great leaders we all know. Do you think Martin Luther King, Jr., couldn't have inspired and engaged a group of eighth graders? Do you think Ross Perot couldn't take a complex topic and break it down into smaller, easier-to-understand parts? Do you think General George Patton couldn't have organized a classroom, laid out expectations, and improved student performance? As former teacher and astronaut Christa McAuliffe said, "I touch the future. I teach." Teaching is indeed the profession that makes all others possible, and I argue that successful leaders got their first modeling from effective teachers. And yet people still recite the mantra: Those who can, do; those who can't, teach. Now I'll add my corollary: Those who can't teach, can't lead.

The skills and attitudes that make some teachers extraordinary are the same ones employed by exemplary leaders in other professions. Of course, the technical body of knowledge is different. But it isn't the math teacher's knowledge of math that makes them a world-class teacher any more than the bank president's knowledge of banking makes them a world-class leader. That knowledge is a prerequisite and nothing else. Successful leadership of students or employees is in the *how*. And the *how* of spectacular teaching or leading other endeavors is strikingly similar. Even in education we often argue that the skill sets are different for a successful principal or superintendent. No, they aren't. The technical knowledge is different, but the ability to motivate, lead people through change, and engage and energize them is the same. Class sessions are now staff meetings. Students are adults. Lesson plans are broad agendas. I found myself constantly reframing my role in other positions so I could see myself as a teacher.

We encourage our best and brightest students to be anything other than teachers. And yet, if they become successful leaders in another chosen field, teachers are exactly what they are!

**Teaching is the profession on which
all other professions depend.**
LINDA DARLING-HAMMOND

THE MAHONEY THREE

ONE: Do a "plate chart" with your staff. Use string to hang a paper plate around someone's neck with the plate on their back, and ask the group to write on it the qualities, strengths, and attributes that person contributes. It's a powerful moment of validation when they turn the plate around and read it.

TWO: Write your own obituary. What do you want to be remembered for in your career? After you write it, put yourself on trial, producing evidence that you exhibit those traits. Are you who you want to be?

THREE: Fill a mason jar with marbles or jelly beans and ask your group to guess how many are in it without discussion. Write down the numbers and average them. Their collective answer will be much closer to the real number than the vast majority of individual answers. It's a powerful demonstration of the way collective wisdom can bolster better thinking and decision making.

Chapter 24

CONCLUSION

The highest reward for a person's toil is not what
they get for it, but what they become by it.
JOHN RUSKIN

NEW YORK TIMES **COLUMNIST** David Brooks often discusses the importance of character. He wrote, quoting Montaigne, "We can be knowledgeable with other men's knowledge, but we can't be wise with other men's wisdom." Wisdom isn't information or a body of knowledge, Brooks suggests; it is the moral quality of knowing what you don't know and figuring out how to handle things despite your ignorance or uncertainty. I like to think I've gained a speck of wisdom through the books I've read, the people I've been privileged to lead for many years, and the experiences I've had (and sometimes just endured).

Many years ago I met a professor at an education conference in Atlanta who had recently won a teaching award. His picture had been in the paper, and he got a telephone call from a lady who saw it. She asked if he had taught senior English in a small Pennsylvania high school twenty-five years ago. He had, and he easily remembered and reconnected with his former student, who now lived in his Southern university town. "I recalled how wonderful that particular class was for me," he said. "They loved to discuss great books we read, and I was sincerely remorseful when the school year ended. I had such a good relationship with them that I was invited to several graduation parties. Of course, I had very little money for gifts. Since they loved books, I decided to give them a handout with summaries of twenty-five books we didn't get to in class but that they should read. I presented each student with my graduation gift the last day we were all together so I could attend their parties without embarrassment."

I sensed his excitement as he told me this story. Any teacher could certainly relate. After all, we all have classes we want to remember and a few we can't forget.

He continued, "I made lunch arrangements with my former student and had a wonderful time catching up. As we were getting ready to leave, she reached into her purse and pulled out a folded piece of paper, purple and smeared with handwritten notes all over it. She smiled, holding the handout I had presented to her years ago, and said, 'I read all these books. When do we get our next assignment?'"

Teaching and leading has been the gift that keeps on giving to me. In education, people remember how you led and how you made them feel.

Brooks distinguishes between "eulogy virtues" and "résumé virtues." Now I read obituaries to look for them. Résumé virtues are considerable achievements: "was chair of," "set the record for," and "was named the." Eulogy virtues are descriptions of character: "he would take the shirt off his back for" or "when she walked into the room with that ever-present smile, people just lit up." Do I have a preference? Yes. Achievements follow from the kind of person you are. How you treat students or staff daily. What you acknowledge. What you expect. All of these define who you are as a teacher or leader. The people you led will first and foremost remember who you were.

Stay connected to those you lead. Remember what it's like to be in their shoes. Consider your "eulogy virtues."

My best lesson: live and lead the way you want to be remembered.

Charles Dickens's *David Copperfield* begins: "I am born. Whether I shall turn out to be the hero of my own life, or whether that station will be held by anybody else, these pages must show." These opening lines spoke to me as a teenager. We each become largely the architect of our own lives. Each life is inherently interesting; the Biography Channel could put together an interesting profile on any person who had lived to adulthood, not just celebrities and other famous people.

We live, love, work, and make decisions that have intended and unintended consequences. In the children's novel *Tuck Everlasting*, Angus Tuck advises the young protagonist, Winnie, not to drink from the fountain of youth as he had. He says, "Don't be afraid of death, Winnie. Be afraid of the unlived life."

This is the story of my life and career: what I learned, what I missed, what I would do again, but better. Most importantly, it's the life I was unafraid to live.

ACKNOWLEDGMENTS

HOW DOES ONE REALLY THANK so many people who contributed to this book? At the risk of unintentionally omitting people, I still want to personally thank those who offered help in such a way that without it, this book would have simply remained an idea. Let me start with both the obvious and largest swath of gratitude: the countless students I've taught from middle school through graduate school and the staff of organizations I've been fortunate to work with over decades. It has been my privilege and honor to learn with you. Without you, there wouldn't be any stories, lessons, or *esprit de corps*.

Special thanks to Meredith Bortz and Dr. Naima Khandaker, two of the most capable staff members I ever worked with, who provided invaluable organization of material, insights, and rewrites; Dr. Larry Long, whose writing expertise, assistance and advice was priceless; Beverly Jobrack, my book editor who used her considerable skills to reshape and edit; Bill Pflaum, a retired publisher who gave me hope, inspiration, and guidance; Jeana Haines, who read, listened, offered counsel, and motivation; Amy Meyer, who is the best teacher I know, for comments, suggestions, and improvements; Leslie Damron and Suzanne Amos, two of the finest JG alum, who provided assistance on every aspect of this work; and Emily Hitchcock and the staff at Proving Press who closed this project.

Certainly others contributed in myriad ways from reading sections, offering commentary, suggesting ideas, encouraging me, or even solving technology problems when I thought I had lost the entire manuscript. Your parts were essential in completing this book puzzle. Much thanks and appreciation to Kate Johnson, Sharon Jones, Larry Miller, Marsha Lewis, Patti Brenneman, Rob Weidenfeld, Judy Mahoney, Candy Jefferis, Nettie Haines, Cliff Hall, Julianne Nichols, Tim Kelso, Paul Cynkar, Barb Leeper, Barb Hansen, Keith Pomeroy, Emily Greenwald, Stan Heffner, Steve Farnsworth, Connie Rath, Brad Mitchell, Mike Gonsiorowski, Bobby Moore and Jim Hyre.

Rarely do any of us achieve anything of substance alone. Thanks again to the people listed here and so many others I've learned from over the years. I'm more grateful than you can imagine.

—Jim Mahoney

WORKS CITED

Achor, S. (2010). *The Happiness Advantage: The Seven Principles of Positive Psychology That Fuel Success and Performance at Work.* New York: Crown Business.

Babbit, N. (1975). *Tuck Everlasting.* New York: Farrar, Straus, Giroux.

Bateman, S. S. (2018, October 18). Management by Walking Around: Motivating and Developing Staff. *Medium.*

Blase, J., & Kirby, P. C. (2009). *Bringing Out the Best in Teachers: What Effective Principals Do.* Thousand Oaks, CA: Corwin Press.

Bridgewater Associates. (2020, September 24). *Principles & Culture.* Retrieved from Bridgewater Associates: https://www.bridgewater.com/principles-and-culture

Brooks, D. (2015). *The Road to Character.* New York: Random House.

Brown, D. (2013). *The Boys in the Boat: Nine Americans and Their Epic Quest for Gold at the 1936 Berlin Olympics.* New York: Penguin.

Buettner, D. (2017). *The Blue Zones of Happiness: A Blueprint for a Better Life.* Washington DC: National Geographic Partners.

Campbell, S. (2017, June 15). 10 Qualities Separating the Extraordinary Salesperson Apart From the Pack. *Entrepreneur.*

Carnegie, D. (1998). *How to Win Friends & Influence People.* New York: Pocket Books.

Carstensen, L. (2011). *A Long Bright Future.* New York: Broadway Books.

Chatterjee, A., & Hambrick, D. C. (2007, September). It's All about Me: Narcissistic Chief Executive Officers and Their Effects on Company Strategy and Performance. *Administrative Science Quarterly.*

Collins, J., & Hansen, M. T. (2011). *Great by Choice: Uncertainty, Chaos, and Luck—Why Some Thrive Despite Them All.* New York: Harper Business.

Comer, D. J. (2015, July 9). *What Relationships Do for Learning.* Retrieved from Connections-Based Learning: http://seanrtech.blogspot.com/2015/07/what-relationships-do-for-learning.html

Cooperrider, D., & Whitney, D. (2005). *Appreciative Inquiry: A Positive Revolution in Change.* San Francisco: Berrett-Koehler Publishers.

Covey, S. (1992). *Principle-Centered Leadership.* New York: Fireside.

Dewhurst, M., Guthridge, M., & Mohr, E. (2009, November 1). *Motivating People: Getting Beyond money.* Retrieved from McKinsey & Company: https://www.mckinsey.com/business-functions/organization/our-insights/motivating-people-getting-beyond-money#

Dickens, C. (1850). *David Copperfield.* London.

Duhigg, C. (2012). Habits: Why We Do What We Do. *Harvard Business Review.*

Editors of Conari Press. (1993). *Random Acts of Kindness.* Newburyport, MA: Conari Press.

Fiedler, F. (1978). The Contingency Model and the Dynamics of the Leadership Process. *Advances in Experimental Social Psychology.*

Freiberg, K., & Freiberg, J. (1997). *Nuts!: Southwest Airlines' Crazy Recipe for Business and Personal Success.* New York: Broadway Books.

Friedman, T. L. (2007). *The World Is Flat 3.0: A Brief History of the Twenty-first Century.* New York: Farrar, Straus and Giroux.

Gallo, C. (2017). *Storyteller's Secret.* New York: St. Martin's Griffin.

Gallup. (2020, September 25). *Gallup Q12 EMPLOYEE ENGAGEMENT Survey.* Retrieved from Gallup: https://q12.gallup.com/public/en-us/Features

Gallup CliftonStrengths. (2020, September 24). *The 34 Ways to Describe What You Natually Do Best.* Retrieved from Gallup: https://www.gallup.com/cliftonstrengths/en/253715/34-cliftonstrengths-themes.aspx

Gallup Press. (2017). *State of the Global Workplace.* New York: Gallup Press.

Gilbert, E. (2016). *Eat Pray Love.* New York: Riverhead Books.

Grant, A. (2014). *Give and Take: Why Helping Others Drives Our Success.* New York: Penguin.

Grenny, J. (2013). *Influencer: The New Science of Leading Change.* New York: VitalSmarts.

Heath, C. a. (2017). *The Power of Moments: Why Certain Experiences Have Extraordinary Impact.* New York: Simon & Schuster.

Kenny, G. (2020, March 16). *Don't Make This Common M&A Mistake.* Retrieved from Harvard Business Review: https://hbr.org/2020/03/dont-make-this-common-ma-mistake

Maturo, V. (2017, August 23). *Majority of U.S. Minorities Regret a Key Education Decision.* Retrieved from Gallup: https://news.gallup.com/poll/216401/majority-minorities-regret-key-education-decision.aspx

Mineo, L. (2017, April 11). *Good Genes Are Nice, But Joy Is Better.* Retrieved from Harvard Gazette: https://news.harvard.edu/gazette/story/2017/04/over-nearly-80-years-harvard-study-has-been-showing-how-to-live-a-healthy-and-happy-life/

Mosley, E., & Irvine, D. (2020). *Making Work Human: How Human-Centered Companies are Changing the Future of Work and the World.* New York: McGraw Hill.

Pink, D. (2009). *Drive: The Surprising Truth About What Motivates Us.* New York: Riverhead Books.

Pink, D. (2012). *To Sell Is Human: The Surprising Truth About Moving Others.* New York: Riverhead Books.

Quinn, R., Heynoski, K., Thomas, M., & Spreitzer, G. (2014). *The Best Teacher in You: How to Accelerate Learning and Change Lives.* San Francisco: Berrett-Koehler Publishers.

Rath, T., & Clifton, D. O. (2004). *How Full Is Your Bucket?* Washington, DC: Gallup Press.

Reeves, D. B. (2020). *The Learning Leader: How to Focus School Improvement for Better Results.* Alexandria, VA: ASCD.

Robinson, S. K. (2006). *Do Schools Kill Creativity?* Retrieved from TED Ideas Worth Spreading: https://www.ted.com/talks/sir_ken_robinson_do_schools_kill_creativity?language=en

Seligman, M. E. (2011). *Flourish: A Visionary New Understanding of Happiness and Well-being.* New York: Free Press.

Siegel, B. L., & Purkey, W. W. (2003). *Becoming an Invitational Leader.* Atlanta: Humanics Trade Group.

Sims, P. (2011, April 5). The Montessori Mafia. *The Wall Street Journal.*

Sinek, S. (2009). *Start With Why: How Great Leaders Inspire Everyone To Take Action.* New York: Portfolio/Penguin.

Sinek, S. (2017). *Leaders Eat Last: Why Some Teams Pull Together and Others Don't.* New York: Portfolio/Penguin.

Waxman, O. B. (2015, January 6). Watch Bill Gates Drink Water That Had Been Poop Just Moments Before. *Time.*

Wheeler, M. (2013, July 29). *Be Happy: Your Genes May Thank You For It.* Retrieved from UCLA Newsroom: https://newsroom.ucla.edu/releases/don-t-worry-be-happy-247644

ABOUT THE AUTHOR

RECOGNIZED AS A DYNAMIC international and national speaker, Jim Mahoney brings more than forty years of real-world experience as an educational leader to inspire, motivate, and challenge audiences of all types. Jim's long experience as a teacher, principal, superintendent, college professor, and launching and leading a large national not-for-profit organization have added considerable value to his skills and expertise in strength-based leadership, motivation, culture and engagement, and change management.

A powerful storyteller, Jim has a natural gift for connecting to audiences' hearts and minds to work together for a common purpose. He has been honored for his work by the International Alliance for Invitational Education, Ohio Federation of Teachers, Ohio School Board Association,

Buckeye Association of School Administrators, and inducted into the Ohio State College of Education and Ecology Hall of Fame. Jim has made presentations throughout the United States, Canada, Ireland, and China. He also co-authored the book *Data-Driven Decisions and School Leadership: Best Practices for School Improvement* and has had several articles printed in state and national publications.

He is currently an assistant professor and Executive in Residence with the George Voinovich School of Leadership and Public Service at Ohio University in Athens, Ohio.

Jim is the founder of RedBrick Hill, a consultancy firm, and can be reached at jmahoney.59@gmail.com.